Contents

Acknowledgements 5
Introduction 7
The Western Front 8
Private James Brown 9
Private Thomas Hardy 10
Private David Gray 11
Private Arthur W. Allison 12
Lance-Corporal F.I. Cannell 13
Private Andrew Byrne 14
Private James Brown 15
Private Lawrence Leask 16
Lance-Corporal Robert W. Jamieson 17
Sergeant Robert Rose Gunn 18
Sergeant James Peterson 19
Anonymous 19
Private James Johnstone 20
Private James Stout 22
Private Arthur Thomas Garrick 24
Private John Peterson 26
Gunner Alexander Campbell 32
Africa 34
Sir Basil Hamilton Hebden Neven-Spence 35
At Sea 44
Leading Seaman Gunner William H. Corkish 45
A. Robertson 45
Able Seaman Andrew Brown 46
Charles Hardy 47
Able Seaman William Slater 48
J.F. 49
James Scott Jamieson 50
James Moffat Scott 50
Captain Henry Mainland 51
Anonymous 52
Charles Hardy 53

Gallipoli 55
Private George Irvine 56
Rev. A. J. Campbell 56
Anonymous (Captain Malcolm Smith) 58
Lance-Corporal William J. Gair 59
The Nurse 61
Nurse Martha Aitken 62
Condolences 66
Corporal Laurence Petrie 67
Lance-Corporal M. Christie 68
Seaman Christopher Coutts 68
Private Laurence J. Cooper 68
Lance-Corporal J. S. Coutts 69
Trooper Edward T. Coutts 69
Corporal Tom Scott 70
Private J. L. W. Erasmuson 70
Private. Wm. T. Spence 71
Sergeant Robert Williamson 72
Lance-Corporal M. T. Cheyne 72
Private George Johnston 73
Robert Jamieson's Letters 74
Signaller Robert Jamieson 74
Index 89

Acknowledgements

Books of this kind are always the product of many kinds of input. The Scottish Library and Information Council runs a Public Library Improvement Fund, and it very kindly provided a grant, without which publication would have been impossible. Numerous people helped in many ways, and the Shetland Museum and Archives and Shetland Library would like to express their grateful thanks to Joanne Wishart, the Bressay Heritage Centre, Douglas Smith, the Leslie family at Laxfirth, Max Ward, Magnus Peterson, Margaret Stewart, Mrs P.G. Paterson, Denis M. Douglas and Bill Douglas, Tony Gott, Isabel Sinclair, Jacqueline Irvine, Annette Jamieson, Magnus Shearer, Vaila Holbourn and Jemyna Henderson.

EARLY DAYS OF WAR - READING LATEST _TELEGRAMS AT NEWS-ROOM_ .

Reading the latest telegrams at the Newsroom. The group includes soldiers of Shetland Companies, Gordon Highlanders. Shetland Museum and Archives SM00059.   Photograph by C. Coutts, 1914.

Introduction

Safely wounded. When the Shetland poet Jack Peterson was recovering from a wound in hospital, one of his correspondents said to him in a letter, "how glad I am to know you are safely wounded." It's one of those utterly true paradoxical statements. He had acquitted himself, known terror, and survived. Most of all, for a time, the war had stopped for him. And we know about this because he wrote letters.

This book of correspondence by Shetland men and women from World War One represents a tiny fraction of those sent. Shetland had two newspapers in those days, the *Shetland Times* and the *Shetland News*. Both published letters from men and women involved in the war, and letters they printed form the bulk of this publication. Others come from the Shetland Archive's holdings, or from private hands.

The letters themselves have an anomalous distribution. They mainly date from the earlier parts of the war. The local papers had stopped publishing letters by 1918. It isn't clear why, but pressures of space and paper supply may explain some of it. It's also possible to speculate on changes in public taste.

Most letters here are from soldiers, while Shetland servicemen were overwhelmingly sailors. The army postal service was formidable, aided by the proximity of the Western Front to home. Troops were able to write home regularly. Shetland's army contingent included a lot of white collar workers, clerks, shop assistants, and so on, who wouldn't have found a place in the Naval Reserve very readily. These men were the army's natural letter writers.

Soldiers were rotated through the frontline and the periods away gave opportunities to write. Support organisations like the YMCA provided writing paper. Soldiers wrote in the anticipation of action, before offensives, and, afterwards, to reassure and inform.

Navy life and the Fleet Mail were rather different. The potential area covered was very large, times at sea could be very long, and mail had to be taken up in port. As the submarine war developed, action took place at short notice, and the end was often sudden. Survivors couldn't pick up personal effects like letters, unless they carried them on their person. Bodies, much less mail, did not survive the ocean.

These letters have a tone, an expression of a different age, when the main way to communicate across distance was the written word, written by hand. We know there are things unsaid, because of the censors, the writers' wish not to disquiet, and the cultural disposition of the time. They can be eerie, fascinating documents, made poignant because we know what happened next. In a number of cases that was the suffering and death of the writer.

The writers couldn't have known it, but their writing involves the reader in an act of remembrance. Write, leave a record, be remembered. Read the letters, make a connection, don't forget.

Angus Johnson

THE WESTERN FRONT

The Princess Mary's Christmas Fund gift 1914, cigarette tin and cigarettes.
Tobacco and cigarettes featured greatly in servicemen's correspondence.
Shetland Museum 02443.   Photo by Billy Fox.

Private James Brown of the 2nd Royal Scots wrote to his wife in Lerwick from the front in September 1914. His two consecutive letters tell of the action at Caudry, Northern France, in what became known as the Battle of Le Cateau. It was the second major battle of World War One, which took place on 26 August 1914. British losses in the fighting on 26 August 1914 were 8,842.

We have had some terrible fighting, and lost a lot of men. We were in a terrible death-trap, and it is a miracle how any of us got out, but we lost about 500 men. The Gordons have only got 180 men left out of a 1000. There has never been such a battle in history. We had to run twice for our lives, but I believe it is about all over now. ... This is the first chance we have had to write since we left home. We have been on the march every day and night, and we are getting a rest for the day, for the men are hungry and worn out. Jock got wounded in the arm, but he is all right. Our Colonel has been killed. I have no more to write, but I will tell you everything if I am spared to come home.

In a subsequent letter Private Brown wrote:–

Our regiment has lost 500 men, and the Gordons 800. John Hunter and Big Rab are missing among them. ... If you can possibly manage to send "fags" every week please do so, as we can't get any "Woodbines" in France. We see some terrible sights here, poor old women running for their lives, and a young woman sitting dying and nursing her child. I don't think this war will last long, but I don't care what we go through now, for we can't get any worse than what we had last Wednesday at the battle of Cowdrie [Caudry]. We lost 2,500 men out of four regiments. Our brigade was the worst cut up of the whole British Army, so I think we have just escaped death, and I don't think we will meet it now. I had to throw my equipment and jacket and run when we got the order to retire, and I lost the photos of you and the children. ... This is all at present, leaving me quite safe and near the enemy. ... Don't forget the "Woodbines."

Private Thomas Hardy (1889-1914) of the Gordon Highlanders, wrote to his younger brother, David Hardy, (1899-1917), Wadbister, Girlsta. Thomas Hardy was to die at Ypres, David was to die accidentally on the s.s. *Bylands* at Calcutta. *The Shetland Times* said the letter was dated from the Expeditionary Force.

Dear Brother

I can't say this is life – it is mere existence. The guns are thundering and shells bursting everywhere. As I am writing the enemy are attacking on our left, about a mile away, as I hear the maxims[1] and terrific rifle fire. We have held this position almost a week under terrible artillery fire.

In the firing line one knows nothing but what's happening to one's immediate front. We may be the only party in the war for all we know.

The rifle fire and artillery fire continue all night, and, to make things more miserable, there is a continual drizzle caused by the heavy guns.

Bullets make a sort of whining noise and shells a sort of seething noise when passing you.

Field Marshall French sent us a note of congratulation which was read to us in the trenches and passed along. He praised the troops under his command for their magnificent coolness and bravery under artillery of such size as never has been used in action on the field before, and how they have borne everything cheerfully. ...

We have been treated with the greatest respect by the inhabitants of the towns. The country round here is cultivated to the last inch, and the people seem to have been well to do. The country through which we advanced to occupy our present position has been thoroughly looted by the Germans, the people having fled, leaving their live stock behind. These we liberated, so that along our front we see cattle grazing and pigs grunting about. The Germans shot all the horses on the farms as they considered they would be of service to us.

It's all right to stay at home and fill the papers with patriotic paragraphs, but really war should be reserved to fiends who are at the last stages of insanity. But we are quite happy, and the glorious traditions this regiment has earned in bye-gone days will, I hope, be further increased. ...

I have put Saturday at the top of my letter, but I have no idea what day it is, only I know it's near the end of the week. Each day follows the other under the same conditions – heavy artillery and rifle fire without ceasing. ...

---

1   Maxims – at this time machine-guns were often referred to after their inventor, Hiram Maxim.

Sergeant David Gray (1885-1917), 5th Scottish Rifles, wrote to his parents in Lerwick, Ogilvy and Helen Gray. He was promoted to Captain in 1917 and killed shortly after.

Our battalion has for the last week been enjoying a much-needed rest about 2 miles in rear of the trenches.

Our ex-sergeants sent out a huge consignment of Christmas fare so we decided that, as the facilities were available, we could not do better than organise a feast at which the sergeants could assemble as a mess for the first time since mobilisation. We would have postponed this function until Hogmanay, but life here is so uncertain, and one never knows what a day may bring forth, so we decided to have a glorified celebration of Christmas and the New Year on the 30th December. Invitations were issued to representatives of the other units of our very serviceable Brigade, and the gathering was altogether a somewhat unique one.

The guests had been enjoined to bring their own tools (cutlery and mess tins). The tables consisted of several doors unhinged from several parts of our billet. The tablecloths were London newspapers which had not found buyers in the metropolis. The seats were manufactured from numerous packing cases, and were long suffering, but it was not surprising that several collapsed during the rendering of one or two of the more animated items of the programme. The illumination consisted of a legion of candles. The piano had been "lent" by some person who was not in occupation of his house.

I shall not weary you with the menu but its quality quite surprised our guests. The programme was varied, and as no one was in a critical mood every item was received with salvos of applause.

During the afternoon several unfriendly shells fell in our vicinity, and speculation was rife as to whether our evening's entertainment would be undisturbed.

I am glad to say we were not subjected to any unwelcome attention. During the evening we had a visit from a party of officers; and the Colonel in replying to the toast of the officers, delivered himself of quite an inspiring address, and made touching reference to our fallen comrades.

The second parcel of which you spoke in your last letter came to hand a day or two ago, and I am much obliged to you for all the good things. Do not, however, send me anything further at present, for in the words of the well-known hymn, "I nothing lack". When we moved to our present billet I was loaded like a "Father Christmas". Our men all affirm they have never discovered till now how many friends they have. The dimensions of mail for our Battalion seems to be a source of amusement at the railhead. I think everyone who is up at the front will agree that the generosity of the people at home has far exceeded our expectations.

Indeed, in some respects this generosity is possibly being rather overdone. At present, at all events, the men have more tobacco and cigarettes than they can smoke, and a few towels or shaving sticks would be appreciated.

I sometimes wonder too whether those who are doing their bit in the Territorial Battalions at home are getting their due share of the comforts which are being so lavishly distributed.

We expect to push forward again in a day or two. There is always a blissful uncertainty about our prospective movements, and a day which does not give birth to a fresh rumour is a disappointing one. A summary of the war information available is published by Corps Headquarters daily, and distributed to all units. We thus get a good idea of how things are progressing in the whole area. This "summary" is, in my opinion, one of the marvels of the campaign.

I don't think I have hitherto told you that an effort is made to give the men a bath from time to time. Our division have a bath-house where 800 men per day can have a hot bath. While the men are performing their ablutions their clothing is treated with a view to exterminating any "undesirable aliens" which may be lodging in their garments. Here too dirty shirts and socks can be handed in and clean shirts and socks got in exchange. The scheme is not without its faults, but this will give you an idea of how much is being attempted for the comfort of the men.

Shetland News, 29 May 1915, page 4

Private Arthur W. Allison (1886-1975), wrote to his parents in Lerwick, Captain George Allison, and his wife Barbara.

May 1915

Last Sunday our troops unexpectedly launched an attack, and before the Germans knew what was on, our gallant lads were among them, using their bayonets freely, clearing off some old scores. Through the day the roar of cannonade was absolutely fearful, and the thought that struck one was, "Could it be possible for anything to live in this?" but seemingly it was possible, as hundreds of Germans were taken prisoners, and I wondered if it was right to take them alive, when one thought of the Lusitania and poisonous gases. One prisoner, I noticed, was a mere lad, and another one an old man.

One day the Germans dropped about twenty shells from their long range guns in the town, the majority falling in fields about 300 yards from us. We had a good laugh at their parting gifts, and thought that was wasteful, as they might require all their shells in the near future.

The civilians who live near the firing line seem quite unconcerned, and go on quietly with their work.

The police are constantly rounding out spies, who go about dressed as tramps and often as priests.

Two things we require is an abundance of ammunition and an unlimited number of men, as we have a strong foe to fight. Surely no man wants dragging-in to such a cause. If only for one moment he realised that it meant life or death, he would jolly soon enlist without making any more fuss about it. Nevertheless some sit back with folded arms and remark that the British will never allow the Germans to reach Calais.

At present we are having beautiful weather, which helps to progress our movements.

Shetland Times, 24 July 1914 page 4

Lance-Corporal Cannell, Sherwood Foresters, wrote a series of letters to his parents. He was Frank Inglis Cannell, son of Revd. William Morrison Cannell and his wife Agnes, Wesleyan Manse, Lerwick. He was commissioned as a Lieutenant in 1917.

July 1915

We came out of the trenches on Sunday, after doing 16 days in. We are not in billets properly yet, but are acting as a kind of general reserve. In a week or so, we hope to go for a rest of ten days or a fortnight. We are all about "beat," and a good number in the battalion were wounded, killed and "gassed." During our stay in, we had some terrible shelling to put up with, and the continual strain is very bad for heads and nerves. Some of us were inoculated yesterday, and on light duty to-day. One of my pals was taken ill on the way back after being done, and I had to "fall out" with him to help him back. He was quite unable to walk without assistance. Both of us had "groggy" left arms, and I had to carry both rifles, as well as help him, it was a rare job I can tell you.

The British army alone must use millions of sandbags every month. Thousands are used in building a hundred yards of trench. Without sandbags, especially in a front line, it would be very unsatisfactory. Trenches are dug out about waist deep, and the parapet built up of sand bags filled with earth. They must be five feet wide to protect the trench from bullets. Thousands of sandbags are also used for barriers, redoubts, barricading houses, etc., etc.

I am sending a 13 lb. shell home, "Little Willie"! A "coal box"[2] is about 100 lbs., and the shelling must be at least 2 inches thick, with very high explosive inside. You can pick out the German big shells at a great distance by the sound K-r-u-p-p with the accent on the K. The French shells also have their distinct sound.

Hope you are well at home, and only wish I was feeling fit myself. We'll roll on our rest, and then we shall be rejuvenated.

---

2 A coal box was a heavy German shell, probably named after the black smoke from the explosion. The writer is using the German Crown Prince's nickname to refer to a smaller calibre shell.

Shetland News, 28 August 1915, page 4

Lance-Corporal Cannell wrote home to his parents again.

August 5, 1915 – ... We were relieved a couple of nights ago after doing another 18 days in the trenches, and have been penned in here, in case we were required at ---------. From what I can gather, we shall be in the thick of it to-night or to-morrow. I hope sincerely that we shall accomplish what we have to do.

I was talking to a man I knew in Nottingham. He has just come back from where we are going to, only 250 left out of 850 in his battalion. He told me some of the fiendish tricks of the Germans. First, they sent over liquid fire, and by these means captured the trenches, and many of our poor chaps were blinded. Our men counter-attacked. They found that the Germans had piled our dead and wounded on the parapet as barricades. I don't think any more is needed to show the awful things they will do. Look out in the papers for news; I pray for our success, as it is a most important position. ...

August 14, 1915 – ... A few more lines to tell you, I am well and safe. I can hardly realise it myself after what we had to put up with. Practically all my friends have been killed or wounded. I am the only N.C.O.[3] in our platoon who went through the whole action. One corporal was left, but he went to the first aid, very soon after the action began. I have to write letters to the wives and mothers of some of my best chums, giving them some idea of how their dear ones met their deaths. After we had taken the trenches, we had to stand 14 hours incessant bombardment, probably the heaviest experienced on this front. Two Generals have sent messages of congratulations both to the Brigade and to the division.

Some of my little adventures were – a shell exploded near me, and lifted me firmly and gently into a ditch full of barbed wire, soaking me up to the waist. Twice I was completely buried, have a slight wound by a piece of shell on right hip, also a chip taken out of a finger with a piece of shell. I have a swollen face, severe headache, and some boils. I have a bandage round my hip but it will soon be all right. As I was racing about, and perspiring all day after my wetting, I must have got a chill. ...

Shetland Times, 18 September 1915 page 4

Private Andrew Byrne (1890-1916), No. 3 Machine Gun Section, Seventh Seaforth Highlanders, wrote to his mother from "Somewhere in France". His mother, Jane Blance, was a widow, his father Andrew Hay Leith Byrne having died in 1890. Private Byrne was to be killed in 1916.

---

3   N.C.O. – a Non-Commissioned Officer, i.e. a rank from lance-corporal to sergeant.

... The parcel came at a very needful time, for, I did not have a "fag" to smoke, and I tell you I enjoyed the old "Woodbines" first class. ... I enjoy the papers you always send me, as they keep me reading – and you need something to read out here. It keeps you from thinking.

We are still resting, but are leaving soon. We have had a good rest this time – nothing but concerts and sports. We had a "church parade" in a field to-day (Sunday) and we got a very good sermon.

I will now tell you about our week's sports and concerts. We had a concert each night for four nights, each Company giving one. I tell you they were as good as any concert that is held at home. There were "great" comic songs, and we had a piano and nearly everything that was needed. The artistes were dressed as women and all sorts of things.

On Wednesday we had Battalion sports. I did not enter for anything except the tug-o'-war. Our gun section pulled against "B" Company, but they were all heavy men, so we stood no chance. The pipers had a competition and they played some fine tunes. We have all enjoyed ourselves this week, but we will be away from here in a day or two.

The Company I was in before had their concert last night, but they did not get it finished as it started raining. It was very good, however, and they had Highland dancing at it.

We are having very good weather, only there was a little rain yesterday.

All the French people are busy with their crops. We are giving the people who own this farm a hand to build their corn. They are very good people, too. ...

Shetland Times, 16 October 1915, page 5

Private James Brown, 2/3 Royal Scots, wrote to his wife in Lerwick from "Somewhere in France", describing his experience at the Battle of Loos.

October 1915

... I have got a bit of a surprise to tell you. I was walking round the trenches the other day and landed in beside the Gordons, and who do you think I should drop on but John Hill. I told him that I had been looking for him since the start of the war. We had a rare old chat about Shetland and various people. ...

I am going to tell you a little experience I had previous to meeting Hill. We had a terrible fight on Saturday morning, last, and we lost a lot of men, but that couldn't be helped. We had to get to the German trenches which we did in quick time, and had them calling for mercy. My job was to run a telephone wire across to the German trenches, which I accomplished; but before we advanced my partners and I were buried in a dug-out which was blown in by a "whizz-bang"[4] and it took us all our time to get out. Then after the Company had held the position

---

4 A term for a high velocity shell, that is one that offered little warning.

for eleven hours by hand-to-hand fighting we had to evacuate the trenches, but we got a splendid name from the General for holding them so long.

The 1st Gordons and the 4th Gordons were very unfortunate as they advanced. The barbed wire hadn't been cut and it was six feet high. The consequence was that they lost a terrible lot of men. However, when we were in the German lines we couldn't get any communication, so I traced the wire back to our own lines. When I was returning to the German trenches I was stopped by the Company coming back, and one chap said – "You can't go back there for the Germans are in their own trenches again;" so I asked him about the telephone operators, and he said they were still in the dug-out in the German lines, so that was a bit of luck for me, as my partners are prisoners, as far as we know, that is if the Germans don't do some of their low down crimes and kill the unfortunate chaps.

The bombardment was the worst fire I have been in since the start of the war. I thanked God when it was over and I was spared. We got relieved for one day and a half, so we are amongst it again, but I don't know for how long. We are in a different position which is very quiet, and long may it keep that way. ...

Shetland Times, 16 October 1915 page 5

Private Lawrence Leask (1895-1916), of the Scottish Fusiliers, wrote home to his mother, Mrs Leask, Fairview, Gulberwick, describing his experience at the Battle of Loos. He was to be killed in action, 3 April 1916, France.

"Somewhere in France"

28th September 1915

Dear Mother,
... By the time you get this, you will have heard about the attack.

On Friday we got orders to put everything we did not need in emergency in our packs, put on name and number, and hand them in to the Company Headquarters. We had warm tea served about 10 or 12 o'clock that night: and also put a day's rations in our haversacks.

About 5 o'clock next morning the attack began. Our guns went off first, but the Germans were not long behind us. Soon we couldn't see any distance for smoke, and we had to shout to each other before we could be heard. About an hour after the bombardment began, our mines went up. Our trenches rocked like a small boat in the wash of a steamer. Our Company was in support of the others. Soon word came for ---- Company to reinforce, as the trenches had been taken but ---- Company could not get up very quickly, as their communication trench was blown up at places, so we went. We had to go doubled up through an advance trench. I got a piece of shell through my cap, which raised a lump on my head, and another piece gave me a slight bruise on the shoulder. About 7 a.m. what could be found of our platoon, along with some from others, was sent out to one of the advance trenches to dig. We were there all day, with the big shells dropping all round. We could feel the ground shaking under us. The trench was a narrow one and we had a job to move in it, and we were only 25 yards from the Germans. We had to do the digging on our knees.

We got relieved about one o'clock on Sunday and went to a farm some miles away. As we lost some men we were waiting for new drafts.

Yesterday, a General came to congratulate us. He said our part of the line had been the strongest. ...

Shetland Times, 23 October 1915 page 5

Lance-Corporal Robert W. Jamieson, writing to his sister, Mrs James Manson, Lerwick, describes the advance at Loos and his experience of being wounded. He had been living south, running a grocery store in Motherwell. When he wrote the letter, he was in Graylingwell War Hospital, Chichester. This may have been Robert William Jamieson (b. 1880, Fladdabister, Cunningsburgh).

Just a note to let you know I'm back in the old country once again, but not so far north meantime as I'd like to be. ... I am rather sorry now I sent you the post-card, as I can imagine you thinking I'm seriously wounded, whereas I'm lucky enough to have got off with a comparatively slight one – a bullet through the left foot. It has done no great harm to the bones either – one slightly fractured and a small one split – and I fancy, from what I hear, that two or three weeks will see them knit sufficiently well to bear my weight. Meantime I'm confined to bed, and I must say I don't like it.

I was hit during the attack on the 25th September. I was lucky enough to get through the charge all right, although our chaps were falling on each side of me under a heavy rifle and machine-gun fire; and I passed through the street fighting in Loos. Pretty one-sided it was, though, as "Mr Hun" was almost demoralised, and, generally speaking, a bomb thrown down a cellar brought the survivors out begging for mercy.

After passing through Loos we took hill 70, and it was while we were being heavily counter-attacked that I was hit. I had to crawl back to the first dressing station (about three or four miles from the top of hill 70), and, as the Germans were sniping the wounded as they were going back to the dressing station. I was perhaps lucky, having to creep, as the grass was fairly long at most places. The last three quarters of a mile was through wire entanglements and over trenches, so it took me about seven hours; but I "got there" at the finish and was lucky to do so. ...

Sergeant Robert Rose Gunn (1873-1917), 7th Battalion, Canadian Infantry. He was the son of Robert Rose Gunn and his wife, Elizabeth Mackay, Laxfirth, Tingwall. He enlisted in Vancouver. In June 1916 he was severely wounded, and was in the UK for six months. He returned to the war to be killed on 9 April 1917, at Vimy Ridge. He is writing to his sister, Margaret Leslie. The letter is the possession of the Leslie family.

France Somewhere
Nov. 10th 1915
Mrs Geo. Leslie

Dear Sister

Just a few lines in reply to your very kind & welcome letter of the 1st Nov. which I received all right a few days ago & was glad to see by it that you were all in good health at L[axfirth] as I am happy to say this leaves me well at present.

In fact I've never been in better health in my life than I've been since coming to the front & we've sure enough had our share of the front up to the present at least a fair share.

I am glad to see that father is keeping so well at present & I sincerely trust he will continue to have good health during the winter & spring.

I also received some papers for which I am really much oblidged. I also received two Shetland papers from Mrs Angus G[unn] also a letter from Angus. I am writing them both by this mail as we are out of the trenches for a spell. Of course pretty soon we will be in again ding dong at it again.

Poor devils of Germans I guess they're getting tired & sick of it all right.

The rank & file of them especially are such <u>slaves</u> I suppose, but all of them high & low were imbued with the idea that one German was better than half a dozen of any other nationality, but I think they have probably learned better by this time.

They say that the Scotch soldiers are the toughest & hardiest fighters of all they are fighting & I quite believe they are correct. If I can I want to get a German helmet & Uhlans lance head to send you as a souvenir but I haven't got one good enough as yet. I have a couple of good shell heads but can't send them by mail – against the rules of the P.O.

I don't have much new of any interest at present. We are having it wet & rather cold at present, lots of mud & water etc. but no snow or frost as yet.

I don't think the winters amount to much in this country. Uncomfortable they may be & wet but no severe cold like Canada. Good job too.

Now you must excuse this short note for this time as I want to catch the out going mail, & my time is limited. So with kind love & best regards to you all at L[axfirth].

I am

Your Loving Brother

Robt. Gunn

Hoping to hear from you soon & give all the news. R.G.

Sergeant James Peterson, Army Service Corps, elder son of Mr James Peterson, Church Lane, Lerwick, wrote to his mother from France.

December 1915

Dear Mother

I am well and getting on fine, although the weather here is very miserable and very cold. We are having plenty of snow, and only one blanket to keep us warm; but I am well used to it now. ... Although miles away from the "Old Rock" I am always pleased to hear how the people at home are.

We are very busy here just now, having plenty to do. There are plenty of the Germans about, too, and their shell fire is never done. We have all received respirators to put over our mouths when the Germans use gas; also smoke helmets to put over the respirators; besides these we have another thing like a false face which we put on when the Germans use their new bombs, called the tear bomb. When they fire these bombs there is some acid in them that makes your eyes run with water for hours, and you cannot fire on them, so that they can advance.

They also have bombs which fire things like steel gramophone needles. I have seen a soldier here the other day that had 25 taken out of his body. They are awful brutes when you think of it. I do hope it will soon finish. ...

Shetland Times, 24 June 1916, page 4

Anonymous. The *Shetland Times* printed an extract from the letter of someone who wanted to be unknown, and has remained so.

We are in the trenches just now and have had plenty of excitement these last few days as we blew up three or four mines in the German lines and our artillery fairly "strafed" them. The German stretcher bearers must have had some work carrying out their dead and wounded. I have had very little chance of sleep for three or four nights up in the firing line as I have had to keep a good look out for fear of the enemy trying to come across, as we are not far from them at this part.

Our bombers wounded one of their men who was trying to get a bomb at a sentry post of ours, but we saw him in time and a chap struck him with a bomb and he lay moaning all night but died during the morning. A patrol of ours went out at night when it was dark, but he was a big heavy chap – about 17 or 18 stone – so they could not get him in. We are up against some of their best men as he was a Prussian Guard that was killed.

After our mine went off, a raiding party went and bombarded their trench and took their provisions.

Private James Johnstone, 7th Battalion, Canadian Expeditionary Force, serving at the Somme, wrote from "Somewhere" to a friend in Lerwick. He asked to know of other Shetlanders in his formation, and for the information to be forwarded via the Medical Hall, Lerwick.

September 1916

... Here we are again; back for a few more days rest. I will endeavour to give you an account of my experiences this last trip which should prove interesting, and I certainly found it myself. We went up several days ago and took up our position in some trenches to the right of the last place we were in. These trenches have a very unsavoury reputation, and are a place where Fritz is very liberal in sending over trench mortars, sausage, minnewerfers and fish tails[5] – a very formidable quartette. They are fired from a very simple weapon (used centuries ago, I think) and their range is not much more than 100 yards. The dug-out is no protection against them.

The first few days were pretty quiet although we sampled his assortment and we only had a few casualties. I was out on listening post duty one night, which was uneventful, although he kept sweeping our parapet with his machine gun and sniping was pretty brisk. We had a little hole, and by crouching pretty low when the machine was coming our way, we were safe enough, although several rifle grenades landed pretty close.

One night – the most interesting – we were all packed up ready and had about three hours to wait, when our commander got information that Fritz was going to blow up a mine. So my platoon was sent down to a support trench to be ready when the mine went up to rush to the crater. The rest of the battalion had likewise different positions and aims. Well, we waited, and there was some talk of its not going up that night, but we had to stay here till the other battalion relieved us any way. It had become pretty dark by now and was rather ominously quiet. I remember the fellow next me saying so, and that he didn't like it – poor chap, he got killed too, shortly after – when suddenly there was a dull roar and the earth began to shake. There was a second explosion a few seconds after the first, and looking up I saw tons of earth and a cloud of fire high up in the sky and our trench rocked just like a boat on a rough day. It seemed to me that we were going to be enveloped at first, and a lot of earth fell round us, but we were all right as far as the mine was concerned.

Fritz opened up with his artillery the second the mine went up, but ours were just a few seconds behind him, and gave him better than he gave us. Then our Captain gave us the order to get up to the front line, as, of course, we expected

5   Various forms of German mortars and grenades, short range explosive weapons used in the trenches.

Fritz to come over and it was too dark to see. Well, we got up there in double quick time, whilst Fritz was shelling our supports all the time. We were all supplied with a stock of bombs and for a while we were pulling pins and throwing bombs at intervals, and others of us were firing over to Fritz's trenches. Meantime our number one company went over and got possession of the crater. I think we gave Fritz a pretty good surprise when we got on the job so soon, and if he had ever tried to come over, he would have had a great reception.

Things quietened down after a time, and we continued to stand to on the fire slip, shooting at regular intervals over Fritz's parapet, whilst the company that were in the crater "consolidated their position." I thought that we would not get relieved that night and would have to wait till next, but at last word came to scabbard our bayonets and move out, as the relieving force were in. We were soon on our way back. Throughout the night I threw over about twenty bombs and fired pretty close to 200 rounds of ammunition, so I was pretty tired and was mighty glad to get back for a decent sleep. Our fellows behaved fine during all this time, and Fritz was pretty lucky in staying in his own trenches, as he would have got a reception that he wouldn't have forgotten in a hurry.

For my own part, I felt good, and was not in the least bit excited or alarmed after the mine incident closed, and we got busy doing something. It seems to key a fellow up somehow when there is something on, and according to my idea the worst time is when you are lying inactive during a bombardment, as I was in my first trip up the line some time ago. To give you an idea of the shock of the mine when it went up, one of the sergeants told me it was about 125 yards long by 75 wide, and about 80 feet deep. Quite a small sized hole, eh? It was an experience I am not sorry for seeing, but I must say I don't want to be so close to one again, nor would anybody else I imagine, what! We had a very small casualty list considering the operation, and I think that Fritz was cut up pretty bad by our artillery and got off a good deal worse than we did.

Well, we are back to our football and cricket and picture shows again, and will be ready to go up pretty soon again. So you see a fellow soon gets used to everything and just takes things as they come.

Shetland Times, 23 September 1916, page 4

Private James Johnson of the Canadian Expeditionary Force wrote again. This time he gave an account of how he was wounded when his battalion went into action on the Somme, 7 September, to relieve Australian troops. The newspaper quoted him: "We were bombed ... until the 10th when I got hit and got out of it."

We were on a ridge and the Germans were on two other ridges. We had taken their front trench, and in front, about 150 yards, we had about 14 stretcher cases in an advanced dressing station between us and Fritz, and down here its a custom for us to go out under the white flag to bring in our wounded (Fritz used red).

Well, the first party that went out a shell landed among them and killed 6 and wounded 4. I went out with the second party and we got out all right. But what a road! From our battalion dressing station to the stretcher cases was about 300 yards, and the ground looked as if it had been ploughed on a large scale. Shell hole overlaps shell hole. Fritz dropped some shells pretty close around us, but we made that trip all right and went out again, but we had hardly got more than 50 yards on our way back. I changed off the stretcher and was carrying the flag when – biff! A whizz-bang hit me a glancing blow on the left thigh making a flesh wound about the size of a six inch circle – didn't hit a bone though. The shell exploded about 30 yards further on after it hit me, but I was the only victim.

A whizz-bang is about an 18lb shell, and is about the fastest shell they throw. It is fired almost straight from the gun, so you can know how lucky I was, and this wound will heal up all right in due time without disabling me at all.

I have to lie on my right side all the time, and I can't sit up, but otherwise am all right.

There are only three of us in this ward who stay in bed. The rest are all in pretty good condition, and certainly make some row.

Shetland Times, 5 May 1917, page 5

Private James Stout, (b. 1898), Seaforth Highlanders. He was the second son of Mr and Mrs C.B. Stout, Medical Hall, Lerwick. He had been wounded during the Battle of Arras, and was writing from Brook War Hospital, Woolwich.

I am going to try and give you a little of my news in France since we left the small village of _____.

We left _____ on the morning of the 9th and marched for miles, passing many a battery of artillery who were all going ahead, pouring shells by the hundred at the Hun. We knew by this time that the Big Push had started. At last we came to a halt and settled just off the road for a rest. We rested there for a few hours and had some dinner, and also got picks and shovels issued out and material for wiring. It was when we halted here that we saw the first signs of the great battle, in the shape of walking wounded cases. There were some really pitiable sights among them, but all seemed more or less glad to be out of it. One poor "kiltie" was coming down the road all covered with blood and mud, uniform in rags, and was being supported on both sides by Germans – big, bulky looking brutes, but who were taking great care in helping this "Jock" along. All those who were questioned as to how it as going said – "Oh, fine;" and that the Huns were being pushed back at a great rate. Next we saw were the batches of prisoners. Lots of 50 and 100 came past about every quarter of an hour all seeming happy and smiling – quite glad to be captured.

We journeyed on from there past what had been our front line trenches, across "No Man's Land", and enemy lines and trenches. What an upheaval had been made by our artillery! Almost every yard of ground had been torn up by our shell fire. We had to proceed by platoons in single file to get across it. This place was still in the range of the enemy's guns and occasionally one would burst round about us. At last we got to the line of trenches where we were to spend the night, and at once started to make suitable dug-outs for protection from shells, etc.

The ground was fairly sandy so we made quite nice little dug-outs. At night we had a brilliant display of star shells and had a few "whizz bangs" knocking around, but nothing to mention. We lived there for two nights and found it pretty cold with snow and no great-coat, only a waterproof sheet. We moved off next morning (11th) and passed through a village which had been used quite recently by the Germans, but is in ruins now. We were then told that our barrage was starting at noon, so we knew when we'd begin. The road we were then on was called "Sunken Road" and as we went forward the height of the bank protecting us on our right got less and less, so that by the time we had got to the top, we had to advance by small rushes, or on our hands and knees, the enemy machine guns spitting just above our heads.

When we had got our proper positions and distances, we waited until the barrage started; then over we went. When our barrage began the enemy machine gun fire was about trebled, and I wonder yet how our fellows managed to get through it, because the bullets seemed to be going over and about my head by the hundred. I kept my steel helmet well down over my face and my head down, rifle with bayonet fixed slung over right shoulder, and my spade in my left hand as a protection for my throat. I had got about 300 yards when something struck me on top of the head, and I fell flat. I was stunned for about 10 minutes, and when I put my hand up expecting to find a gash in my head, lo and behold! there was nothing but a small lump about the size of a shilling! I ventured to take off my helmet because the bullets seemed to be flying at a higher range and found that a bullet had penetrated my helmet, followed the curve of the crown inside, and found a way out over my back or shoulder. It gave me a bit of a shock to think of the narrow shave I'd had. By this time our chaps were a good bit ahead, so I got up to go on the way again, but only got 50 yards or so when I went down again with a bullet through the right knee. That settled it that time no more going on for me.

I began to think what was the best way to get back, but found I couldn't crawl because the bone was broken. I managed to get part of my iodine and field dressing on, and then, with the help of my shovel placed the right foot and leg on top of the left, and with entrenching tool handle as splint, wound my puttees round both my legs, binding them together. When I had fixed that I found that I could, with difficulty, crawl a little by lying on my back, reaching back my hands and pulling my legs after me. I had barely got 100 yards when I had to give it up as hopeless. I came across another fellow who was wounded, lying on his face. In the afternoon the snow began to fall, so I put my waterproof sheet over me and lay patiently waiting for stretcher-bearers to come. They came once or twice but took some cases from further down the field. We lay, and lay, and still the snow came down, but no signs of anybody.

When night drew on and lights and flares went up, I thought we'd been forgotten about altogether, but at last they did come about 12.30 at night, and I was taken to 1st Dressing Station in the village we had passed through. The first thing I got was a cup of hot Horlick's Malted Milk, which I did enjoy, seeing that the only thing I'd had that day was a few small biscuits in the early morning. From there I travelled by motor ambulances and trains until I landed at 13th General Hospital, Boulogne, crossed the channel in the "_____", and landed in this hospital on Sunday night (15th), so that about ends my tale.

I still have my souvenir helmet – have carted it about with me everywhere I went, so wouldn't like to lose it now.

This is a nice big hospital, and we get everything possible done for our comfort, and when we are able to get up and walk, and are allowed out, we can go out from 2 till 7.

There are only one or two other Scotchmen here, nearly all the others are Canadians or other regiments. A Canadian, two beds away from me, said there was a fellow called William Ward, who came from Burra Isle, Shetland, who was in their battalion, 7th Canadians, and that he thought I might know him.

Have to stop now as this is a beastly awkward position I'm writing in, lying on my back.

Shetland News, 10 May 1917, page 8

Private Arthur Thomas Garrick (1888-1973), Kamloops, Vancouver, was the son of Peter Garrick, Ollaberry. He joined the Canadian Expeditionary Force and was wounded at Vimy Ridge, 9 April, 1917. Pte. Garrick settled in New Zealand after the war.

I posted a card the other day by which you would know that I came safely through the big scrap, albeit I got slightly hit. I got hit on the night of the 12th, on the fore-arm and the thigh, with shrapnel, but didn't "go out". It was only mere abrasions which made me a little stiff and sore. The officer was going to send me out the following evening, but the scouts reported the further withdrawal of the Germans, so we advanced a matter of a mile or more. We secured our hold on a couple more of small towns, but the enemy machine-gun fire arrested our further progress for the time being.

Next morning we went forward to the attack again on another town – a pretty little place – seemingly bigger than anything we had yet taken. We were forced to advance in the open on a nice flat plain, but the enemy had the place well trenched and wired, and he shelled us quite considerably with a couple of light field batteries and a 5.9 battery. His machine-guns and snipers were fairly active, too. While lying on the ground trying to look as much like a blade of grass as possible, and wishing I could crawl altogether under my steel helmet, another piece of shrapnel again banged me on the left arm, nearly on the same place as the first wound, and bruising it somewhat. It was just enough to make me useless there, so I went to the dressing station and thence to the hospital. When I took off my equipment and saw where the shrapnel had cut my tunic and perforated big holes in my mess-tin, I marvelled how I'd come through so lucky.

You will have read in the papers the glowing accounts of the big push, as well as the Canadians' achievement in capturing Vimy Ridge. To show what Fritz thought of his position on the Ridge, two days before we made the attack he put up a big sign on the barbed wire in 'no man's land', where we could see it. The sign read, _____.

So, naturally, if we were inclined to be pessimistic, we would wonder what contraption he had rigged up for us.

But when the fateful moment came, when there was just enough light to know that daybreak was coming, and that beautiful barrage opened up, there was nothing to it. You didn't know the thing had started, hardly, until you were in the German front lines. I only realised that I was taking prisoners after several had put up their hands, and I had signed to them with my bayonet to keep on going towards our lines and keep their hands up.

That barrage was, I think, the most wonderful music I ever heard. The bombardment had been steady and heavy all night, and wasn't all one-sided. Fritz was shelling quite heavily also. Then, at daybreak, there was a lull for three or four minutes, and then it seemed that every gun in the world opened up. Where we had assembled in the front line the noise didn't seem so great. I think the quantity of guns in continuous firing seemed to dispel the volume of sound. It was just a quick, nervous, totoo, on the whole very steady, but sometimes thinning off, and then all coming in with more and renewed energy. That's how it sounded; I can't say how it looked. I was too close to it.

You wouldn't believe how close we followed that barrage. You could hear the shells whistling close overhead and the shrapnel bursting directly overhead. I saw some of Fritz's flares go up – all colours of the rainbow, and all kinds of designs: white star shells, red flares, double green ones, strings of sausages, and golden sprays. He was frantically calling for help from his artillery, but there was little or nothing doing. They didn't know where to shoot, and I think we must have silenced the majority of the German batteries with the opening of the barrage. I understand that between gas shells and shrapnel we kept the enemy gunners out of action. The enemy tried the same thing but to no avail. His observation was 'on the blink'. We never saw a 'plane of his that day.

We gained our objectives with no trouble, practically speaking. My company captured three machine-guns that I know of. Just before we'd got our second objective we fell in with a very persistent sniper. Bombers finally worked round him and disarmed him. They found cartridges in his rifle with the bullets reversed,[6] and also in his pouches. Judgement was summarily executed with two of his own bullets.

Besides taking all our objectives ahead of schedule time, we kept pushing forward until the enemy was placed in such a position that he had to evacuate a big stretch of territory. It was while helping the process of evacuating Fritz that I came in for my souvenirs. The weather has been continually against us, but the German is still on the move. If we could get the artillery up faster we could move him faster.

I suppose I'll be out of hospital again in a day or two. I am quite well. Donald Sutherland, who used to be a policeman (in Sandwick), is in the same ward. He asks to be remembered to you. He got hit on the knee, but is able to limp around. So, hoping everybody is well, I'll stop, with love from your son, ATTIE.

Private John Peterson, a.k.a. Jack Peterson, Seaforth Highlanders (1895-1972). Letter to Miss J.J. Campbell, 34 Burgh Road, Lerwick. Jack Peterson was wounded in France on 3 May 1917, and again on 18 October 1918. He worked as customs officer, a photographer, and as a poet. Politically, he was a Communist. He published a volume of poetry about the war, *Roads and Ditches*, and wrote an unpublished novel partly based on his wartime experiences, now in the Shetland Archives. The poems mentioned here are "When I Come Home," by Leslie Coulson (1889-1916), a war poet, and "I Shall Not Ask Too Much", by David Morton, U.S.A. (1886-1957).

Shetland Archives SA2/618. Original in the possession of Mr Douglas Smith.

Ward D4
Mill Road Infirmary
Liverpool

May 23rd 17

Dear Miss Campbell

I cannot thank you enough for your cheery letter and nice parcel and those things you so kindly sent me in France. Of late I have grown rather weary of reading my friends tales of parcels sent across the Channel, and thoroughly appreciate your more substantial way of breaking sad news. Two very belated letters were all I received among my pay weeks in France: and I have come to the conclusion that to send anything to anyone at the base is scarcely worthwhile. It arrives there all right, but no endeavour is made to find the owner nor has the owner any opportunity of getting it for himself: at least that was the state of affairs as regards the Seaforth's mail at the 18th I.B.D.[7]

---

6   The German army used a blunt-ended bullet against British tanks, for armour-piercing. It was sometimes used against infantry.

7   I.B.D. Infantry Brigade Depot.

Jack Peterson, 1940s. Shetland Museum Y00221.

Photographer Robert Ramsay.

I am exceedingly sorry to hear of Jimmy Inkster's death. When I arrived at the Base his was the first familiar face I saw, and although I did not know him to speak to in Lerwick, we of course met like old friends over there. And for almost a fortnight we were together in the B.B. camp.[8] Then he went up the line, one of a merry "mob" of Gordons singing and cheering as they all sing and cheer. We would meet again in Lerwick (with a smile) – just as Karl said it, and Jamie Sinclair and all those others. One feels almost ashamed to have come back to the kindness and comforts and all that in Blighty.[9] Nor did I know Tammy Aitken in Lerwick, although I saw many of his fine photographs and often wished to make his acquaintance. Indeed, I looked forward to it in going to France, as he was in my old platoon in the 8th Battalion. Very much against my will I was sent to the 7th. I fear the 8th must have caught it badly as I understand Jamie Blance is also wounded, and in the paper I see that my old company captain has been killed in action.

In considering the figures given by Bonar Law[10] in comparing the casualities [*sic*] of the two great pushes, there are several things to be remembered. The Arras push was carried out very quickly compared with the Somme advance; the former was a great battle, the latter a series of smaller actions. In the Arras battle the number of men in action <u>at the same time</u> was greater by many times than any single battle of the Somme, and though the percentage was down so very considerably, our casualties for the time were enormous. That Shetland has suffered so heavily lies probably in the fact that in a space of two weeks the two Scottish divisions and the 51st (in which are the 1/7 Gordons) were in the thick of it.

By all means copy the poems I had the pleasure of sending you. If there be one thing in poetry that brings disappointment, it is that when one has found a gem one can so very rarely turn to one's neighbour and ask him, share the joy. A hundred to one he will not understand.

I have other poems of Leslie Coulson's, all of which are good, and which I shall remember to take home with me. But there is one other I am sure you will like, and which I shall enclose. There is a sad irony in that such lines as these should have been written by a man who fell in France.

"When I come home, from dark to light,
And tread the roadways long and white,
And tramp the lanes I tramped of yore,
And see the village greens once more,

---

8   B.B. Camp. It's unclear what this abbreviation means, but possibly Brigade Base.
9   Blighty. A services term for the British mainland.
10 Andrew Bonar Law. The Conservative Party leader in World War One, and Chancellor of the Exchequer in the British wartime coalition.

The tranquil farms, the meadows free,
The friendly trees that nod to me,
And hear the lark beneath the sun,
'Twill be good pay for what I've done,
    When I come home!"

I have seen fragments from Laurence Binyon's[11] work, but cannot remember having heard of the poet Thomas.[12] When I was leaving for Cromarty last time I was home, I ran across "Poems of To-day" in Mr Morrison's shop and I humbly confess I sinned to the extent of trying to persuade the young lady behind the counter to sell me a copy – all in vain: the wrath of the teacher of literature fell not on the head of some poor innocent up at the Institute.[13]

There is a little snap of poetry by one David Morton,[14] which I have carried round since Christmas, always hoping to find more by the same author. So far I have failed to find his name mentioned anywhere.

It was quoted by Robert Blatchford as expressing the sentiment of the Clarion Fellowship[15] at home to the Clarion boys in the trenches.

"I shall not ask too much beyond the grave;
Just some dear common things that living gave
       x x x x x
I shall want little paths of woods and walking,
And those same friends at evening and their talking
Under oil-lamps, in queer quaint smoky places –
(I would not lose their voices and those faces).
Those I shall ask beyond the narrow grave,
And time for them – which living never gave.

"And time for them –" very fine, is it not!
"The Isles of Thule"[16] is wonderfully fine.

I have often felt that Shetland might be the subject of a really great poem, and the more I knock about – or get knocked about – the more I feel it. There have been many poems "Thule" but this one you send me comes nearest of all I think of deserving the title. I'm sure we can feel proud a Shetland boy wrote it – but, who but a Shetlander could write "The Isles of Thule"!

---

11 Robert Laurence Binyon (1869-1943), author of "Ode to the Fallen."
12 Probably the Welsh poet Edward Thomas (1878-1917)
13 The Anderson Educational Institute, Lerwick.
14 "'I shall not ask too much'", *The Forum*, 55, 1916, p.340.
15 A socialist society organised by Robert Blatchford, editor of the *Clarion* newspaper.
16 William Thomas Porteous (1886-1917), from Ollaberry, a Shetland poet unpublished in his lifetime, who died of meningitis while in the Navy.

This poem, however, deals rather with an aspect – the wild majestic grandeur of West-side cliffs and West-side ocean breakers. There is yet the Shetland twilight, the Shetland summer-night – if one may call it night. It calls for such a poet as wrote the "Lake-Isle of Innisfree".[17]

Thule – the wrath of the gods, the holy quiet of the current of rest and peace; aspects and the contrast of aspects: it is something I am waiting for. And the poems you send me gives me to think I may not have to wait for ever.

Magnus Robertson is in France. The day I came to Liverpool, where it could have been quite easy for him to come and spend some time hours with me, he was put on a draft and went off about a week ago: I had post-card from Rouen and expect a letter daily. I have got some very amusing letters since I came to hospital, one phrase in particular keeps coming up in my mind – "Dear John, I cannot say how glad I am to know you're safely wounded" – which sums up the situation quite nicely.

My wounds are almost healed, but my left foot keeps me in bed, at times allowing me to course round in a wheeled chair. And it will likely be so until I get the shrapnel extracted from the leg, which the doctors are apparently in no haste to do. All the same I'm having quite a good time, and so long as I don't feel any bad effects the doctors may take their time.

> With many good wishes
> Believe me
> Yours very truly
> John Peterson

Shetland Archives D9/58/4

Writing as 'Private Pat', Jack Peterson submitted a letter to the Clarion newspaper column 'Letters from Clarion Soldiers', published on 6 September 1918.

DEAR WINIFRED,[18] — I have it in my conscience that I promised to tell you of a big push. The push itself does not matter, it was like other pushes, very stupid, and of course we got there and beyond, but—well some day I may be fortunate enough to take part in a real Beach Thomas[19] battle, when I shall tell you about it. But of the days before I *will* tell you.

It began on the train when we went blazing southward in a manner marvellous to one knowing the usual behaviour of French war trains. Rumour whispered of the Germans advancing on Paris, and of the old division flying to the rescue. An historic ride, crammed in cattle trucks, anywhere and anyhow, getting there,

---

17 W.B. Yeats.

18 Winifred Blatchford, daughter of Robert Blatchford, publisher and editor of the *Clarion* newspaper. Her name is also spelled *Winifrid*.

19 Beach Thomas – William Beach Thomas, a Daily Mail war correspondent whose despatches did not always find favour with the rank and file of the army.

while people waved and cheered. Women hung with flowers the railway bridges to greet us flashing by, crowding overhead to shower down bouquets. And the answer was a cheer in a welter of smoke and sweat and Highland pibroch. Until we came to a land where we were strangers, and people gazed in wonder, rushing from their beds in the early morning and out into the streets to wonder at us marching by.

By night we marched, and when the sun blazed fiercely we slept in the cool of some great dim wood, and at evening when the sun was near the edge of the wheat fields and the shadows were long we descended upon the nearest village. "Descended upon it"—Cæsar's was a happy phrase! Down winding pathways, through the vineyards, in sections and platoons, to some sleeping village at the foot of the hills. Then we swarmed over it; we filled it to overflowing. Every street, every lane, every barnyard and barn, every hayloft, shop, café, and estaminet bright with Highland tartan.

People pulled down their windows, or rushed out of doors to marvel at the strange new soldiers who had so suddenly taken possession of their little town, and who made themselves so much at home. Clustering round the fountain in the market place to wash their brown faces and browner knees, or sitting on doorsteps to clean rifles and long gleaming bayonets.

Children looked on dumbly, and did not shout "Cigarette! Bully-beef!" as their little brothers of the north had learned to do. Girls in groups stood apart and discussed the strange garb of the barbari. Only old women came forth and jabbered, as old women must, and laughed as old women will. The excitement grew.

Then came the band, out into the market-place. A dozen pipers, half-a-dozen drummers, and the pipe major and the drum-major—all pretending to be very indifferent and fed-up. The villagers flocked around, waiting for—for what? They were rather doubtful; something very exciting, certainly. Then the colonel tapped the drums to make sure they were quite all right; the drum-major tapped the drums to make sure they were all right; and the drummers stood very still and very rigid, waiting. The pipers blew their pipes to readiness. The excitement became intense. The drum-major held aloft his baton; the big-drummer raised his drumsticks, the side-drummers raised their drumsticks, and the pipers stiffened their lips. Breathless silence!

The baton dropped, the drumsticks crashed down, the drones brayed, the chanters skirled. For a moment those astounded people hesitated; then the band swung down the street, and the village went mad. Oh, they are very honest in their mirth, those French villages. Young and old. The children rolled in the dust shrieking with glee; the boys hooted and ran; the girls screamed and clapped their hands and followed; women grabbed up children and hurried in pursuit. French soldiers threw their caps in the air and jumped on one another's backs; Italian soldiers embraced one another; and all followed. All followed the band, up and down and round and round. And the pipers played as they had never played before, and the drummers bear their drums as if their lives depended on it. Pibroch, strathspey and reel, until the air shrieked and quivered in clamorous echo.

Mad nights they were, until the sun sank and the bugles sang "Lights Out." The villagers went home to their beds. And with the dawn, weary and footsore, kilos and kilos away, towards that land from whence flowed streams of sad-eyed refugees, were we. And as we lay down in the woods, no doubt the people of the village talked of, and laughed at, the strange manners of the strange men who had come so suddenly and had so swiftly vanished in the night. So, until we left the world behind and straightened the "impossible" salient.

If it was a great journey blazing southward, what it must have been for that tiny fragment going back, their work accomplished and more than accomplished! I can hear them: "Why can't those French people have a little common sense! Flowers, flowers, flowers! What about a bit of rootie?"[20]

Years hence old women will tell of the kilted men and their passing; and in the sunny fields by the River Andre will stand crosses that mark a battlefield.

I may even begin to like soldiering; and who knows, seeing the war is going to last for seven years, but that I may become a lance-corporal or something before it finishes! And give up scribbling stupid letters, and polish my boots and buttons instead. It *would* be grand.—Yours, etc., PRIVATE PAT.

Gunner Alexander Campbell (1890-1918), Royal Garrison Artillery. He was the son of Alexander Campbell, Burgh Surveyor, and his wife Mary Ann MacDonald, King Harald Street, Lerwick. He had been teaching in Hamilton. He wrote in anticipation of sudden, violent death. He died of pneumonia, following influenza, and never reached France. The letter is in the possession of Douglas Smith, Lerwick.

Hamilton. June 17th 1917.

My Dearest Mother.

I suppose that if any eye but my own ever rests upon these lines, it will mean that my own are closed for ever. Well, where many good men have led we must not fear to follow, and I know that despite your sorrow you would not have other mother's grieving in order to keep your own safe. God grant it otherwise, I love life, and I know it will mean much to you, but if it must be, I hope I shall be not found wanting. But it is not of myself I think – I am not afraid of death; it is of you that are left I think, yours is the hard task, to you is left the bitterest portion, and for your sakes I hope the fates are kind.

However, this is really meant to be a business letter, to explain things to you. I have left everything to dad, as that is the simplest, & I know that what is his is

---

20 Rootie – probably a reference to tobacco.

yours. I leave a rough estimate of my assets. Outside my insurance policy, you should have about £100; more if the superannuation is paid. See that you lose nothing – they've had their money's worth out of me. Regarding the so-called bond of £50 I gave you, the facts are these (& this is the chief reason for this letter). There is no bond, and never was one. As you will see from my P.O. Bank Book I had at Xmas 1916 nearly £70 in hand.

You may wonder how I acquired it, but that scarcely matters, except that it was all gained outside of my school salary, mostly by hard work, too, and I can assure you, honestly (This by the way). It was all with a fixed purpose, which if you read this I shall not have lived to fulfil, but a purpose that I hoped to secure before long, & might already have done if there had been no war.

However – I wanted to give you the £50, for the war had postponed the cause of its collection for some years, but I thought you might not take it with the same freedom if you knew it was my savings: hence the story of the bond. I told Mr Crawford of the supposed existence of it, in case you should ever happen to mention it to him & he should look surprised. So I should have no debts of any kind against me, and it may be of some consolation to you to get a little of the cash I have might have lived to give you. I know you will not look at it in that light, but I shall die ever so much happier in the thought that you will not suffer in that respect, at any rate. But let's hope all this has been unnecessary, & that I can burn it before long. God keep & bless you, dear mother, and dad, & all the girls, & Johnnie, & all my friends – you will ever be in my thoughts – Goodbye all. Alex.

AFRICA

Sir Basil Neven Spence, circa 1936. Shetland News, 21 January 1937.

Sir Basil Hamilton Hebden Neven-Spence (1888-1974), retired from the Royal Army Medical Corps as Major in 1927, and was later MP for Orkney and Shetland. He left a body of letters written to his mother during the war.

Shetland Archives, D12/200/5

Extract from a letter, dated 12 October 1914, Khartoum, Sudan.

... all the other E.A.[21] officers (have) been recalled from leave. They had an exciting time: a P & O liner was chartered by the British Government to take back all officers on leave in England to India Egypt and other stations. There were 700 on board including 15 Generals. They were packed like sardines and the E.A. contingent slept on straw palliasses in the cockpit. No lights were allowed to be shown at night. A British Cruiser accompanied them to Gibraltar where they were taken over by a French cruiser. They crept along the north coast of Africa, going inside the islands, whilst the cruiser stayed in the offing, outside the islands. The Goeben and Breslau were in the Mediterranean at that time, so they had to be very careful; it would have been a good prize for the Germans. ...

Shetland Archives D12/203/4

Extract from a letter dated 14 March 1916, Sudan.

... Just a scrawl to say I have arrived safely at El Obeid (pronounced "obeyed") ... This is a big place, but very godforsaken country. I don't like the look of it at all and I should say it is not half so healthy as Yei. Nothing but sand & scrub wherever you look, & quite impossible stuff to walk in. I believe when the rains come in July grass springs up everywhere. So does malaria.

I have charge of the civil & military hospitals here, drawing £5 a month extra pay for the former. I had a look round them today. There are a good many troops here at present, but of course most of them are further up country, at Nahud and such places. The Sirdar[22] is there just now, & is expected here in a few days. There is to be a lot of fuss and a levee at which we will all attend. Savile, the Governor, is giving a dinner party in the evening; there will be 24 of us at it. ...

There is also polo, golf and tennis. I am not going to play polo, as it is an expensive game. The golf course has no tees, greens, holes, or grass, but still we can play on it; you decide the "hole" as you go along, probably a clump of grass or a palm tree. ...

---

21 Probably an abbreviation for "Egyptian Army."
22 The British Commander in Chief of the Egyptian Army.

Shetland Archives D12/201/7

Extract from a letter dated 16 March 1917, Jebel Midob, Sudan, to his mother

... It is strange what small things decide the turn of events. The army of the Mahdi[23] which overran the Sudan & swept the British & Egyptians out of the country had not a fraction of the training, equipment & other advantages that Ali Dinar's[24] army had. The Mahdi opposed & totally annihilated an army 5 times the size of that which went against Ali Dinar. A.D. too had an army with tradition having constantly waged organised warfare for the last 20 years with the semi-independent states of Tama, Masalit, Kubbi, Kabga, etc. What then was it that made A.D.'s 10,000 fade like smoke in the first engagement? Simply the fact that there happened to be no one on their side who could fan the flames of fanaticism which was the Mahdi's strongest weapon. He built his army starting on religious principles whilst Ali Dinar's was purely an instrument of tyranny. ...

Shetland Archives D12/203/5

Extract from a letter dated 18 March 1916, Sudan.

El Obeid is a rotten hole though it is supposed to be one of the nice stations in the Sudan: I hate the heat & the sand & the flatness, & I dislike the Arabs. They are always gassing about the prestige of the Briton here, but I don't see much of it; the Arab is an ill-mannered surly brute, & I should imagine they hate us from the bottom of their hearts. ...

We are having a great tamasha[25] here. The Sirdar came in yesterday & Savile, the Governor, gave a dinner party to about 25. And tonight we are doing the same in the Mess. This morning there was an inspection of about 2000 E.A. troops here; they are very smart on parade, & at drill could not be beaten by the Guards. He rode round the barracks, hospital, etc, & then held a levee afterwards. ...

Shetland Archives D12/200/12

Extract from a letter dated 17 May 1916, Kordofan, Sudan.

... It is funny to see the British tommy in these surroundings. Having been spoon fed to the highest degree in France he is suddenly pitchforked to this country where everyone has to fend for himself, & it has beaten him absolutely. I don't wonder it appals [sic] them; few people in Britain realise that Britons ever live

---

23 Muhammad Ahmad al-Mahdi (1844-1885), an Islam inspired Sudanese leader who rebelled against British rule with some success, taking Khartoum in 1885.

24 Ali Dinar (1856-1915), a Sultan of Darfur, Sudan, who rebelled against British rule in 1915.

25 Tamasha. A party, but the term is probably from a Hindi word meaning "fun" or "play."

their ordinary lives in such wastes. Groves, a senior major in the Army, who is running the flying part of this show, never imagined anything like it; and Castle, another major, who has knocked about India for 17 years, is completely flabbergasted. As for the young R.F.C.[26] officers, they need teats still. I really [believe] that without us here more than half of the British & their officers would be dead by now. They would never have reached here at all. ...

Shetland Archives D12/200/13

Extract from a letter dated 26 May 1916, Kordofan, Sudan.

Just a scrawl as I am very busy. We heard yesterday Kelly had got into Fasher so the flag now wags over another 100,000 square miles of Africa. They had some scrapping but only 2 British officers were wounded I believe; one who was in an aeroplane in the thigh, & the other in the foot. The aeroplane fellow was caught in a habub after dropping bombs on Fasher. A habub is a violent gale & sandstorm. It is quite dark like smoke, & fills your mouth & nose, & chest & eyes with stinging sand. He managed to get back to Abiad. Next day they continued & an aeroplane saw the people scattering in all directions from the shells. One body fleeing was accompanied by a huge white flag; this was Ali Dinar. The flying man swooped down, dropped a bomb & scattered the lot. A.D. has not been caught yet, but the others are all coming in with their news. It is a good finish to a well run show. No other army has lines of communication 400 miles of soft sand with very little water at intervals, to work over, & supplies are carried on camels.

Must stop now. Very busy with another convoy of sick

Shetland Archives, D12/203/13

c/o The Postmaster, Khartoum
El Fasher
12th December 1916

My Dearest Mother
I think my last letter was from Chind on my way here. I arrived on the 29th after a very pleasant trip with Vandeleur's[27] company of the Camel Corps. However no sooner had I got in than I was told to leave that day at 2 pm with three cars and go 120 miles S. W. to meet Huddleston's column returning from Dibbis after the slaying of Ali Dinar. I had to make a water reconnaissance for him as he was bringing in 500 prisoners and refugees, and I was also to make arrangements as regards smallpox which had broken out.

---

26 R.F.C. – Royal Flying Corps, the air component of the army.
27 Probably Major T. B. Vandeleur.

The road was reported to be more or less cleared for 80 miles and a party was working on towards Dibbis. I was to take my chance of camels from them, as they were known to have 3 for carrying water, and continue my journey by camel. I got away about 4 pm as I had to wait for the mail. The first 10 miles was over cotton soil and fairly good going, though bumpy over the khors.[28] The next 10 was all undulating sand hills consisting of very loose sand so the going was very heavy resulting in a good deal of shoulder work. It was dark before I reached Abu Zereiga so I stopped on the top of a rise for the night.

I went on next morning but was quite certain we had got on the wrong track and I saw smoke far over on the left; we went straight across country and after 3 miles or so found Abu Zereiga. From there the track was fairly well marked and the going good (There are no maps of these parts yet) and we buzzed along at a good 12 miles an hour passing fulas (stagnant pools) at Kulkul, Abdel Baigi, and Sumit; on these I shot a lot of duck, and after estimating the available water made a tour through bad bush to the east to look for a fula called Fua el Naga said to be about 8 miles away. I found it all right after a rough ride and as it was a very fine large one with good shade and duck I decided to stop for lunch.

After that I went back to Sumit and struck S. W. on a 12 mile run for Juba; this was good going as the grass had been beaten down, big stones put on one side, and stumps taken out. I fetched up at Juba all right but one of the drivers started a bad bush fire by throwing out a cigarette, and about 200 yards in front of it we got a puncture. The grass of course is as dry as tinder and the fire leaps along at several feet a second so it was rather awkward. I ran 2 cars on across a wide sandy khor where the fire would probably be checked; it was obvious we could not get the other one done before the fire reached us so we brought it on too across the khor and then changed the tire.

The chief feature in Juba was the Juba or tomb of Ali Dinar's mother a large burned brick mosque, or gama as they call a mosque in these parts. I slept at Juba after visiting the Bir Watain, or wells, 3 miles away. On the first I sent one car back with my water report, and then pushed on to Keila to see the wells there; we were now getting into the foot hills of Jebel Marra and the going was much more rocky in places; ahead could be seen the mass of Jebel Marra looking up, very imposing and not unlike the foot hills of the Himalayas. Many of the villages through which we passed were deserted; I was passing along the route of Ali Dinar 's flight from El Fasher, and he no doubt picked many followers from them whilst others fled to the bush either from fear of the neighbouring Arab population or us. At Shavau there was another red brick gama, rather like a small lighthouse in shape.

Soon after leaving Keila I found the working party, about 50 of the late soldiers and slaves of Ali Dinar, under an officer of the Military Works Department. Here

---

28 Khors. A kind of seasonal watercourse.

I had to abandon the cars and fortunately got 3 camels from the officer and was able to push on in the afternoon; I did 17 miles that night passing the wells on Khor Gabra. On the morning of the 2nd I hoped to do another 17 miles, and get to Dibbis with a short skid in the evening.

However after about 7 miles I met some E.A. soldiers who told me Huddleston and his whole party were on the road behind them. Soon they began to come along the wives, concubines, children, and eunuchs of Ali Dinar, some walking, others on camels, ponies, donkeys and cattle; it was a wonderful sight. Many had on beautiful silk clothing of all shades and colours and carried ferocious looking silver mounted swords. These I found afterwards were the harmless people, his harim, and younger sons chiefly. Presently along came a band of tattered looking individuals under guard; these were lately soldiers, about 50 in number.

Next I met Huddleston, and Therburn, whilst not far behind were the political prisoners. They consisted of two lots; 4 sons and 2 nephews were in one party mounted on ponies in single file, with a man of the Arab B[attalio]n between each. They were dressed in magnificent coloured and embroidered silks, but of course had no arms.

The other party consisted of Wad el Sheikh and Abd el Kheir the former in a broad striped orange and red silk and the latter in an orange silk. They are supposed to be more or less fanatical, and were under close guard. Wad el Sheikh is a very fine looking man mixed Fur and Arab blood I should think but possibly a Dongalawi; he is supposed to have been the chief counsellor of Ali Dinar. The rear of the whole party, which stretched for 3 miles along the track was brought up by a guard of startlingly white coloured Arabs to prevent raiding by Arabs along the road. This was a constant source of mild trouble as every night they appeared and carried off a few women or cattle and baggage.

I turned back with Huddleston of course and we stopped for the morning at Tamad el Kedada, a sandy khor in which they were soon all busy digging for water, which they got 6 feet down and very muddy, also not much of it. There was an M.O. with the party, not a very bright specimen. The first thing I did was to drive all the people together, no small job as they were spread over a large area. I inspected them all and found seven cases of smallpox, 1 being a soldier. I sent the lot back to Dibbis with the M.O. I forgot to mention that a feature of the party was Mahommed Fadl, the 5th son of the Sultan, with a broken thigh due to a bullet wound; he was being carried on an angarih a native bed, by the aforementioned party of ex soldiers.

We left Tamad el Kedada in the afternoon and slept half way to Khor Gabra where we camped next morning. Camels were dying at the rate of 6 a day which rather complicated matters and the people were abandoning kit all along the road. In the evening we got to where the 2 cars were; here I took over Mahommed Fadl and had his bed lashed crossways across the back of the open car. I brought his mother along in the other car and was very glad I did so as she nursed him well. We reached Juba that night, the 4th, and pushed on to Sumit next day, arriving at Kabga in the evening of the 5th where we slept.

The people were not at all inclined to believe that Ali Dinar was dead but the sight of the wounded son rather convinced them. However whilst congratulating me as a member of the victorious government they were careful to condole very humbly with Muhammed Fadl in case of any mistakes. I got into El Fasher on the 6th and took the wounded man to the hospital.

I will have more to say of the late Sultan and his family in another letter, and much to say about Darfur and El Fasher as far as I have seen them.

In the meantime I have just got orders to go as S.M.O.[29] of the Northern Patrol and leave El Fasher on the 20th December. Vandeleur is in command, with Hobbs as the other Camel Corps Officer, and Walker in charge of Maxims. Boyce of the Survey and Hall of the Sudan Civil go too. There are 250 rifles, all Camel Corps, and about 500 transport camels. We are going into a country that has never been traversed by a white man before and is entirely unmapped. We will go, if we get as far, to a point 400 miles N.W. of El Fasher where we will establish communication with the French in the French Congo; it will be a historic meeting if it takes place. There are two tribes to go through whose reception of us may not be altogether amicable, and at one place we may come into contact with the Senussi.[30]

As we are going away from El Fasher I will get no mail for 6 weeks anyhow and you need not be alarmed if you don't hear from me for a month or six weeks, as communication may not be altogether easy. I am extraordinarily lucky to get in this show, but I can't say I have ever had to grouse about my luck. I hope to goodness my ammunition will turn up before I go. I know it has got as far as Nahud. Otherwise I have no arms and will have to carry half a dozen spears according to the custom of the country. I got seven very nice ones the other day from one of the eunuchs.

We are each carrying one month's supplies and another month's on the transport company. It would be a strange thing if British Officers in France had to supply all their own food, but here we will be 800 miles by camel from the base of supplies and we don't get a bean from the government.

I have just sent in my service return and find I have now over 2 years double service in; that means that all service to gratuity, pension, etc., now counts as if I had joined at 21 instead of 23, eg I could if I liked retire at 41 now on £365 a year.

I hear my 4 Uganda tusks are at last on their way down.

The cold here at night is most intense; on trek you never take your clothes off and even then under five blankets you shiver like an aspen. The sun is only

29 S.M.O. – Senior Medical Officer.
30 Senussi. A Sufi traditional poltical-religous group spread between Libya and the Sudan.

pleasantly warm by 9am and at 5pm you need a woolly of some sort on. It is a tangible cold, like the intense dry cold of the Punjab.

Thanks very much for the hankies which you say you are sending for Christmas; they are a very good idea as I blow my nose in my fingers as often as not these days. I hope they will get me before I leave as there is only one more post due in and if it is late as it usually is we will miss it. It is a pity you did not send the plum pudding too as they're always very popular and good things are not easily come by in these parts. I have a huge one which cost me 6/- at Fortnum and Mason; it is worth about 10/- as it stands now; I am taking it out on the patrol.

I am not surprised that Bertie does not write very often; he has been out a long time now and living in one spot for any length of time does not encourage the art of composition. I can assure you you are the fortunate amongst a thousand mothers in the matter of letters from us. I have not met anyone in this country who writes long letters; the great majority cover half a sheet of notepaper once a fortnight or month and merely say that they are still alive. I think you take far too gloomy a view of life. We may presume that Dad has had his fair share of troubles, about half and half in fact hasn't he? You have had the agony and he has had the bloody sweat. Anyhow it never comes out in his letters. You never seem to add up the credit side to strike your balance. Does it never occur to you that you are amongst the fortunate to have four sons alive as I write instead of perhaps 1, or none? Also that whilst you may pay 2/- a stone for potatoes I could not procure them here if I offered 200/- a stone.

If there is any debt owed to people who live in countries like this it is the debt of cheerful letters. You may be certain of one thing and that is that they are the only cheerful things that ever occur. It is about impossible for people at home to have any conception of the kind of existence that makes our life in a country like this. It is an eternal struggle with crassly ignorant, negligent, superstitious and unmethodical people, to try and produce order and cleanliness in their lives and surroundings. If you saw the average man passing through Cairo on his way home after 12 or 15 months you would say what a nervous looking wreck he is, what a dreadful climate he must have been living in. Not so; you can put 9/10 down to the daily round and 1/10 down to climate. You ordinarily go through as many severe trials of temper in a morning as a man might reasonably expect to have in a year at home. Two men have gone home mad this year, yet there is nothing surprising in it, though like the rest of this army they were specially selected as having been adjutants of their regiments and were healthy normal men when they came out. Others have died of diseases that they would probably have overcome had they been attacked in full vigour instead of after a grinding year which has turned their fibre to pulp.

There are two products of life in this country as seen amongst the elderly officials with rare exceptions (1) a curious looking wreck, quite abnormal, who works in a high gear and takes 8 hours to do what a fresh Englishman would do in 2 and who thinks of his work when he is not working and dreams of it at night, (2) the lethargic type who have given up the struggle.

The great thing that strikes you in this country is the way Englishmen rise above the surroundings and endeavour to maintain a highly conscientious standard of duty in very adverse circumstances. Syrian, Greek, Armenian all sink to the level of the better class native without an effort at resistance. I cannot imagine any Englishman sinking so low that he would willingly consort with the Greek community in a Sudan town.

Well well it's nearly 4 hours past my usual bed time so I must stop.

Love from your affectionate son

Basil

Shetland Archives D12/203/14

Extract from a letter dated 25 December 1916, Sudan.

... I organised the dinner which we ate tonight:

Ful Sudani Soup
Toast
....
Salmon & Lobster
Mayonnaise Sauce
....
Roast Leg of Gazelle
Potatoes, Cabbage
....
Doves en Casserole
Peas, Mushrooms
....
Plum Pudding
Brandy Sauce
....
Sardines on Horseback
....
Dessert
....
Coffee, Liqueurs

Champagne (1/3 of a ½ bottle each), Beer, Brandy, Kümmel, Crème de menthe.

We had all our tables together with a huge fire on each side; it was a very cheery meal, & as each of our cooks only had one or two dishes to cook it was very well cooked.

Shetland Archives D12/201/2

Extract from a letter dated 12 January 1917, Furowia, Sudan.

The French don't appear to have behaved much better than the people here spending their time in cattle raiding over the border; the people don't seem to have much use for them but seem very glad to see us. I have no doubt they tell the French the same tale mutatis mutandis.[31] These people like all other blacks I have come across call us the red people, not white, which is perfectly correct. Of course we are all very sunburned. ...

We are a cheery looking crowd of ruffians all growing beards & mostly in rags. I started clean shaved, moustache & all, & kept it up for a week, but the moral effect of unshaven people round me sapped my fibre & I succumbed. It is an extremely difficult matter to shave every day when you only get water every 3rd day or so, in fact water is too precious. It is extraordinary how soon you become reconciled to a dirty existence.

What on earth I am to report in at the Adj. General's office in Khartoum I don't know. I simply have not a rag; my helmet is a battered wreck and I have no sleeves in my tunic, both my boots are burst, my shorts are patched & my leggings are dropping to bits. ...

---

31 *Mutatis mutandis.* A Latin phrase, meaning "the necessary changes having been made."

AT SEA

Royal Naval Reserve mobilizing at Custom House, Fort Charlotte; sailors walking up Harbour Street. They were addressed by Lt. Col. H.C. Evans, who announced the formation of the R.N.R., Shetland Section. Shetland Museum SM00060.
Photo by C. Coutts, 8 August 1914.

Leading Seaman Gunner William H. Corkish (1879-1918), in the Shetland Royal Naval Reserve, wrote to his wife in Law Lane. The *Shetland Times* noted that the letter had been opened and read by the censor. He was originally from the Isle of Man, and had settled in Shetland. He was to die on 26 February 1918 when HMS *Exmouth* was torpedoed.

H.M.S. --------- 26th November – A few lines to let you know that I am keeping in the best of health. ... Well, as you will have read in the papers about us ----- British ships, I need not tell you much about our ship. On Monday week we were over in Belgium, and on Monday, as you will have seen by the papers, we bombarded a town. We knocked it all down, and set fire to the whole town, and left it in a heap of burning ruins. If you have not read the papers about it, the name of the town we bombarded was Zeebrugge. It is on the Belgium coast. The German opposition was feeble to us ----- British ships, and we had a gay hot and lively time for a while, but when it was over how happy and pleased we all were to find on arrival back that ----- the crews and ships were all safe and in good spirits. We were glad we came out scatheless. I hope this war and trouble will soon be over. Remember me kindly to all enquiring friends.

Shetland Times, 16 January 1915, page 4

A. Robertson. According to the newspaper, he was in the Royal Naval Reserve, and from Ulsta in Yell. He is otherwise difficult to identify. His account is close to that given in the *Carmania's* log. The incident is the Battle of Trindade, after a Brazilian island about 500 miles east of Brazil. Both vessels were armed auxiliary cruisers, the German protagonist being the SMS *Cap Trafalgar.*

Shortly after 11 a.m. on 14th September, 1914, we observed a vessel on our port bow, and, on nearer approach, we saw that there were three vessels – one a large liner, and the others, colliers. The latter had their derricks "topped," and were probably working when we hove in sight. Before we had "raised" their hulls they all made off in different directions. The large liner was apparently about our own size, with two funnels painted to represent a Castle liner.

After running away for a while the larger liner turned to starboard and headed towards us. Our speed was about 16 knots and hers about 18 knots. We fired, at 8,500 yards, a shot across her bows, and she immediately opened fire from her starboard after guns. We opened with all our port guns and the firing became general.

We were now within good range, but most of her shots were going high; consequently our rigging, masts, funnels, and ventilators, all suffered. By this time she was well open on our port side and both vessels were firing rapidly.

Owing to the decreasing range, her machine guns were becoming dangerous, so our ship was turned away from her and range opened for our starboard battery to throw it into her as hard as we could. Some of our hits were seen to work havoc among the enemy's deck fittings.

Both ships were now on fire – almost ablaze. She was well on fire forward, and was taking a list to starboard from the effects of our shells. One of her shells passed through the cabin under the fore bridge, and, although it did not burst, it started a fire which became worse and worse. No water being available, owing to the fact that our main was shot away and the chemical fire extinguishers proving of little use, the fire got such a firm hold that the fore bridge had to be abandoned, and the ship commanded from aft, the lower steering gear being used.

At this time the enemy was on our starboard side, with a list to starboard; and at one hour and forty-five minutes from the firing of our first shot, she capsized and went down, bows first, with her colours flying.

It was some time before we could get the fire under, and this necessitated our keeping the ship before the wind, so that we could not go to the assistance of the survivors. Some were seen to get away in the boats, and they were picked up by one of the colliers which was standing by.

The enemy, before sinking, was in communication with some German cruiser, and, as our signalman observed some smoke in the northern horizon, afterwards seeing what was supposed to be a cruiser's funnels, we went off at full speed in a southerly direction.

After some hours steaming at 22 knots[32] we got in touch with the Cornwall; we asked her to meet us as our ship was unseaworthy and practically all our communication and navigation instruments were destroyed, rendering the commanding and navigation of the ship difficult and uncertain.

On the 15th, at 4.30 p.m., the cruiser Bristol picked us up, and escorted us to Abrolhos [33] Island to anchorage, in order to effect temporary repairs.

Seventy-nine projectiles and innumerable smaller shells had hit our ship, making in all 304 holes. We also had five men killed, four very badly wounded and 15 slightly wounded out of a crew of 421 hands all told. The four seriously wounded men died on the 15th.

Shetland Times, 30 January 1915, page 4

Able Seaman Andrew Brown, a sailor on the cruiser Kent, wrote to his wife in Lerwick from the Falkland Islands, on 11 December.

We left Portsmouth on 12th October, and went to the West Coast of Africa. We have had splendid weather all the time. We came from the West Coast to here on the 6th of this month to meet a German fleet of five ships, which we did on the

---

32 This is probably a misprint in the newspaper. The speed was actually much lower.
33 Abralhos. A small group of islands off Bahia State, Brazil.

8th. We sighted them in the morning, so we were not long in getting under way and pursuing them. I am very glad to say that we managed to sink four of them, but one of them got away. None of our ships were seriously damaged, and our casualties were very slight. We had 6 killed in our ship, and the Glasgow had one. ... It is rather cold here, very much like home weather. I hope we will be coming a bit farther north; then we will get some warm weather. I really do not want to go into action again for a long while, for it is a very serious job, and a pitiful sight to see so many men and ships being destroyed. ...

We have had no war news from home for a while so I don't know how they are getting on. I know the Germans have had a big slap here.

Shetland Times, 14 August 1915, page 4

Charles Hardy (1891-1916), son of Thomas and Janet Hardy, and brother of Private Thomas Hardy, killed at Ypres, 1914. He was second officer on board the transport *Euphorbia*. He was later lost when his ship, s.s. *North Wales*, was torpedoed off Penzance. Writing to his parents in Girlsta, he said he was well, and wished the war was over.

It was great seeing the Turks trying to hit us ... their shells were dropping all round, and one of them sent some splinters on to our deck, and another grazed the ship's stern. We could hear the shell coming – a sort of buzzing sound like a bee. We could see the firing line plainly. I was on shore three times. There have been several ships struck, and one that had Turkish prisoners on board had seven of them killed by a shell. I saw an aeroplane being brought down. Everybody has praised the transports for the risks they have run. While lying here for a few days we had always a few aeroplanes round. ... The heavy gunfire shakes our ship, as if we were doing the firing.

Shetland Times, 13 November 1915, page 4

Charles Hardy wrote home again, to his father.

... I have just returned from Suvla Bay (the new landing on the Gallipoli Peninsula) after being there a month. We were shelled daily, but they could never strike us although several shrapnel shells burst overhead and the bullets came on board. We were under cover then, and fortunately nobody was hurt.

The Turks are certainly rotten shots. The last night we were in Suvla Bay they trained a battery of heavy guns on the harbour. Two warships were hit, but no damage was done to them. The submarines are getting very active about this part of the world now.

We are loading all sorts of things from the battlefield – casualty kits, etc. Well, I don't have much news at present. I hope to have a letter from you before we leave here, so that I can answer it. You better not write until you get a letter from me, so that I can give you the address. Kind love to all.

Able Seaman William Slater (1881-1915). From Trondra, he was a sailor with the Currie Line and was made a prisoner of war in Germany at the beginning of the war. He was to die in a sanatorium in Charlottenburg, 29 April, 1915. The *News* said his "kindness and generosity were truly exceptional." The letter itself reflects a deep religious belief.

Englanderlager, Ruhleben Hospital, April 17. 1915.

My dearly beloved father and mother, sisters and brother, – This is just a few lines to comfort you all, should it please our Heavenly Father to take me to himself, which I think may not be long, as I have been much worse this last week, though in the midst of every kindness, both with doctors and nurses. But, dear ones, only for my darling wife and little children, I leave all without a murmur. Christ has been all in all to me. It is not death, it is just a parting from things below. It is just going to be with Christ, which is far better, and eye hath not seen nor ear heard, neither hath it entered into the heart of man, the things that God hath prepared for those that love Him. Oh, that I could tell you the great love of our Heavenly Father through His Son to me during my illness.

You would think I must have had a lonely time (there have been dark hours in every life), but some of the sweetest hours I ever spent, have been in hospital in holy communion with Our Heavenly Father, and should it be His will that I have to leave you all, it is just me going home before. I trust, as unbroken families we may meet where there will be no partings and no shedding of tears. I have just been thinking what a great difference there must be between those who know Christ and those that know Him not, as I lie here and realise that for me death has no sting, the grave has no victory. Oh, that all would seek the Lord and follow Him. It is a grand life. When we are in health we often are ashamed to call ourselves Christians, and often do wrong, yet think of the love of Christ for us. It is just glorious, when we feel that life is drawing to a close, so do not sorrow over much, for the dear Lord may come at any moment for all His children. Dear ones, seek Him, try to live near to Him, and the more you cast yourselves upon Him, the more you will realise His love. Give my love to all my uncles and aunts, and my dear little nephews and nieces, and I can only say to them, seek the Lord ere it be too late.

And now, my dearly beloved father and mother, do not grieve for me. You know you are all in the evening of life, and we shall soon meet again; so when it is dark around you and you are cast down, look up – the Master will lighten the gloom, and I leave you, as Christians, in His great care and love. I know you, as Christians, will look to Him and not be turned away.

Give my love and sincere thanks to the Leslie families, who have done so much for us at all times, also all the neighbours round about. And now I commend you to God and the word of His grace, which is able to build, establish and strengthen you, and may the divine peace of God, which passeth all understanding; keep your hearts and minds through Jesus Christ. Give my special love to my dear brother Tom and tell him when he can afford, to ever remember you and my dear little ones. Dear father and mother, sisters and brother, it is just a parting for a little while, then we will meet to part no more - Your loving son, WM. SLATER.

Our Father which are in Heaven, help my loved ones not to sorrow for me as those who have no hope, for if we believe that Jesus died and rose again, even so them that are fallen asleep in Christ will He bring with Him, when He comes to take all His loved ones from earth.

Shetland Times, 20 November 1915, page 4

J.F. Known only by his initials. A Shetland sailor on the Naval Reserve, "J.F.", was interned in Groningen, Holland. He wrote to the *Shetland Times*, responding to a report in the *Times* of London, saying that they were "independent and did not require any help from home."

Of course, we admit that we are not so badly off as the boys in Germany; but I don't see why we should be left out altogether. As to our food, there are a good few men here who can only get one meal a day. The rest of the food they have to provide for themselves; and most of the men have to depend on their ten cents a day, so we manage to get three meals a day, but have to go without food from four in the afternoon till eight next morning, and we have to be content with a parcel from our wives once a month. Out of the ten cents we get per day, we have to provide our supper; so you can see we have two classes of men here – a few who have means to provide anything they want, and those who have nothing, get nothing. I think we should get a little help somehow, and that we should not be left out altogether, as it is coming a bit hard on the married men here to depend on their wives to send out parcels. When they see it stated in the papers that we are independent, we will receive nothing but our ten cents, which can only buy one white loaf.

Of course, the Dutch people have done everything they can to make us comfortable, and we have nothing to complain about regarding that.

I hope you will publish this letter in your valuable paper, and that some kind souls will "do their bit" towards keeping the Scotch-Shetland lads, who are now interned at Groningen.

Shetland Archives, SC12/36/14, page 116

James Scott Jamieson (1878-1915), Second Mate of the ship *Active* of Dundee. He was the son of Andrew Jamieson and his wife Coventry Jamieson, Longhill, Bigton. The *Active*, an old Dundee whaler, foundered off Stronsay, Orkney, on the night of 24/25 December 1915. This is his will. The document was in a bottle that drifted ashore near Stronsay. Note that the question marks in brackets were made by the legal clerk.

Finder Please Post Andrew Jamieson Longhill Levenwick Shetland. Dear family this will be my last letter to you to the N & E of Lerwick God bless you all as he has given me strength to die my soul is resting on the finished work of Jesus a navy boat passed us and we told him we were sinking I have been under the boat at right side trying to get the water out and (?) pulled (?) and again the water is at my knees on the cabbin (?) don't murn for me meet me in heaven Mother Father Agnes Andrew Ann Margaret Coventry again God bless you all I leave everything among you that (Signed) James S Jamieson Ann Henderson Father if (?) family.

Shetland News, 13 January 1916, page 4

James Moffat Scott (1886-1959), the son of Captain Scott of the ss. *St. Rognvald*, wrote to his brother, McGowan Scott. The vessel was probably the *Glengyle*, 9,395 tons, of the Glen Line, sunk 240 miles east by south off Malta on 1 January 1916 by U 34 commanded by Claus Rücker.

I suppose you will have heard by now of our little bit of experience. It was pretty hard luck, after being 40 days on the run, to get blown up on the last night.

We sighted the submarine about 4.30 p.m., and at the same moment he opened fire on us. The first six shots fell short, so we thought we would give him a chase. He kept banging away, and the shells started falling ahead. Then they came fizzing aboard. The first came flying past my head, and if I hadn't ducked I believe it would have put a hole through me. The same shell fell on the fore deck and scattered things a bit.

Another one fell on the after deck and knocked the head off a Chinaman. Poor fellow, after his head was off, his body continued running along the deck.

By this time we saw it was useless trying to get away, so the skipper ordered the boats out and stopped the ship. We signalled that we had stopped, but he took no notice. Another shell fell in one of the boats while it was being lowered, killing one of the sailors and wounding three Chinamen.

At this time I was on the bridge hoisting a signal when suddenly there was a terrible crash and a feeling as if of an earthquake. I looked round and half the bridge had gone, so I thought it was time to get out of it. All the lifeboats had left the ship's side. I got my boat away all right, but the Chinamen, getting a little excited, shoved off.

The Captain, mate, second engineer, wireless operator, and myself were left on board, so we went away in the small dinghy. By this time the submarine was getting close up to us, and the shells were falling amongst the lifeboats. We made our boat fast under the stern of the ship for a while, but it got rather hot there so we shoved off.

The submarine came right along side the ship and put a torpedo into her, and five minutes from then the good old -------- went down stern first. It was a German submarine. He came alongside our boat and asked for the master, and took him on board the submarine and made him sign a book, and then disappeared.

We were lucky, being only about two hours in the boats when, after showing distress signals, we were picked up by the -------. While being taken to ------ we were chased by another submarine for about half an hour, but, having the speed, we got clear of her.

I met Bert Duthie, son of Mr Duthie, late fishery officer at Lerwick, now on his way to do "his bit" as the saying goes. Of course we lost all our belongings, but young Duthie refitted me. The engineers of the ship that picked us up were very kind, and we are now in the hands of the British Consul.

The Company had our effects insured for £50, which is better than nothing, but I have lost a lot more than that.

Shetland Times, 18 November 1916, page 5

Captain Henry Mainland (1876-1932), writing to his relatives in Bressay. The girls in the pictures referred to were his nieces. He had an interesting career at sea, at one time being employed by the Philippine government as an inspector of vessels. His ship, the *Lanao*, was sunk off Portugal. It was the subject of diplomatic correspondence between the U.S.A. and Germany, on the basis that it was an American vessel. Germany maintained that it had been sold by Findlay-Millar SS. Co., Ltd., Manila, to Hannevig Brothers, of London, and so was British flagged.

When the submarine crew boarded the ship to blow her up with a bomb, they ransacked my cabin, even taking the picture frames from the walls, including nice Japanese frames containing photos of the Stout girls and others. What I took myself on board the submarine they also kept.

We were all well treated on board the Norwegian ship, and Captain Johnsen of the Tromp shared and shared alike, though he was short of provisions, and on our last day together we had no flour left. He claims that it was us that saved him, as he had been held up earlier in the day, and the submarine had been so busy that they had not had time to attend to him. When it got dark, he was making best his escape when we overtook him in the submarine, and he thought when he saw the submarine that he was doomed also. The Commander of the submarine was thinking all the time that the Tromp was a Spanish ship, and he did not find out that she was a Norwegian until he came up to her.

Our boats had been lost, so the submarine Commander had to put us somewhere, and he put us on board the Norwegian. The submarine was in a great hurry as vessels' lights had been sighted and he feared that torpedo boats might be after him. He had been in action the same day with a British steamer which had wireless. That steamer arrived all safe at Valencia.

Shetland News, 21 February 1918, page 4

Anonymous. This sailor's letter is to his brother-in-law in Lerwick, and it was the second time he had been torpedoed. The vessel lost was probably the *Lofoten*, 942 tons, managed by W. Coupland and Co., torpedoed about off Start Point, Devon by UB-38. The U-Boat itself had been lost to mines by the time the article was printed.

I have often been to write to you lately, but times with me have for the last three months been very strenuous. So time went on and culminated on the 3rd instant, when I was torpedoed again. We got it at 11.30 at night and the ship disappeared inside one minute, so there was no time for boats to speak of. Fortunately the starboard boat was just at the water when the ship made her last plunge, but was too late to shove off, and the eight men in it were thrown out owing to the boat being carried down by the suction.

I went down with the ship but came to the surface again, and found myself close to the overturned boat. I scrambled on to the bottom thereof, along with three others, and spent the long winter night there, unless for moment when our grips were torn off by the heavy sea running, but we managed to crawl back on top and hold on again until we were rescued by a patrol at 8.30 a.m. on the 4th.

From start to finish it was very trying, but the first hour and a half were worst, as we could hear the cries of our shipmates all round and could render no assistance, after that all was quiet save for the moan of the wind and the wash of the sea.

Towards morning, we were all somewhat spent and beginning to see rose coloured, and I and the one sailor saved had to hold on to the one fireman saved, as he was too far gone to hold on himself; and do you know when the patrol was approaching us I threw away my coat and everything I could get off and stood by for a jump, and at the proper moment got up, sprang, and got on board the trawler almost without assistance, and then threw my three comrades on board, or rather tried to help – I don't suppose I was much use, and there were plenty of willing hands there without me.

Not bad for an old chap, was it, after nine hours buffeting by the billows.

Well, well, you will be getting tired of this lay. I get home a week to-morrow, and M— and B— say I am to go no more to sea, and it is perhaps a good thing for me that we cannot get too much food, or I believe I would be killed with kindness. So I have made up my mind to lay back for a little while at any rate, although I am feeling quite all right, in fact I feel nothing wrong at all, only I cannot help thinking of the seventeen fine young men who went down (the four saved were the oldest men on board).

Shetland News, 5 October 1916, page 2

Charles Hardy (1891-1916), writing home again. The *Euphorbia* was a vessel of 3,837 tons owned by the Stag Line of North Shields. It was sunk about 56 miles off Algiers, by U-39, commander Walter Forstmann, on 16 July 1916.

Just a few lines to let you know I am well, and hoping this will find you enjoying the same. I sent a letter from Algiers, but believe the mail-boat was sunk, though I do not know whether my letter was on her or not. I will tell you a little about my experiences. We were torpedoed on 16th July. It was a fine Sunday morning at the time. We got no warning whatever. Both our starboard boats were blown away by the explosion and firemen on watch were killed. The forward port lifeboat got jammed by the concussion, and we had to lower it on the harbour deck. It got stove in there, but finally floated off. We were 5½ days in the boat before being picked up, and we have been nine days in hospital in Algiers, but are homeward bound now. We lost 19 men altogether. I brought in 11 with me, and the Captain brought 28 with him. We were floating on our tanks, and I could only take seven men in the boat and towed four men on a raft. We left Algiers on a French mail-boat on Friday and sighted a submarine on Saturday evening. It fired at our escort, but had to submerge.

We never saw the submarine which sank our steamer until we were in the boats, and then only the periscope. He never showed his hull at all. It was my watch below, and I was asleep at the time. Well, we have to expect these things in war time, and it is one consolation to know that you are serving your country.

From Lady Jellicoe

STATION, KILDARY.
TELEPHONE Nº 3 KILDARY.

June 29ᵗ

TARBAT HOUSE,
KILDARY,
ROSS-SHIRE.

Dear Mr. Anderson

I went to see your brave Son in the Naval Hospital at Queens ferry on Saturday you will be glad to hear from me he is very comfortable & everything is being done to ease his pain. I am glad to be able to inform you he is making good progress.

Yours truly

Gwendoline Jellicoe

A letter to the family of Francis Anderson, Hillside, Bressay, wounded at Jutland. Signed by Gwendoline Jellicoe, wife of Admiral Jellicoe.

Courtesy of Bressay Heritage Centre.

54

GALLIPOLI

Private George Irvine, Australian Infantry.
Photo courtesy of Mrs Jemyna Henderson.

Shetland News, 22 May 1915, page 4

Private George Irvine wrote to his brother, Henry Irvine, Glenfield, Dunrossness. George Irvine was one of the older recruits into the Australian army, being born in 1875 at Hillwell, Dunrossness. Nothing is known of what happened to him after the war.

Egypt

1 May 1915

Dear Brother

... I suppose you have seen in the papers about us landing at the Dardanelles. Well, we had a very difficult task, but we succeeded; only our losses were very heavy. The Turks had been waiting for us a long time, and they knew when we were going to force a landing.

I was in the first boat that landed in the darkness, and we had to rush them with the bayonet. By daylight we had them going. I got a slight wound in the thigh, but I will be back among them in a week or so, as the wound is healing very fast. We lost mostly all our officers.

As you will see we are back in Egypt, where all our hospitals are. We are well treated.

We don't know how many we lost, but we know that the 9th, 10th, 11th and 12th (3rd Brigade) had the heaviest casualties. The Australians make great fighters. I will never forget the first bayonet charge. The Turks cannot stand the bayonet, and their shooting is very bad. It may take some time before we beat them, but now that we have got a footing we are all right, and we have the Navy with us all the way. It will be slow work on the sea on account of so many mines. ...

Shetland Times, 27 November 1915, page 4

The Rev. A. J. Campbell served as Chaplain to the 1/5th Highland Light Infantry. He had been Church of Scotland minister in Lerwick from 1902-1909.

1/5th H.L.I.
157 Infantry Brigade, 52nd Division
Mediterranean Expeditionary Force,
2nd November, 1915

Dear Sirs

I am now in my fifth month of residence on the Peninsula. Things are somewhat different from what they were when I came. The fierce shelling to which we were all subject when we came has died away considerably, though recently the Turks seem to have had a very slightly improved supply of munitions.

As time has gone it has been possible for us to add a few comforts – not many – as we are far from home. We live in a desert, or rather in what has been turned into one. There are no villages or houses here, and the troops live in dug-outs. People at home have perhaps an imperfect idea of the tremendous strain at the Dardanelles. The whole area occupied by the Allies is so small that in an hour an ordinary walker could walk from the first line trenches to the landing place, and in a rather shorter period could walk from one side of the Peninsula to the other. The men come down in their turns from the fighting trenches to the "Rest Camps," but in the camp they are subject to shell-fire, so much so that it is said not inaccurately that the firing line is the safest place in the Peninsula.

But we get accustomed to all this, and go about as freely as at home. The average soldier is a young man, and is not easily depressed. To see him at meal times, or during a baking expedition is a cheerful sight. A shell went into a store of Army biscuits (very, very hard) and reduced several boxes to fine powder. A man who had narrowly escaped, rubbed his chin and remarked:– "I spent two hours yesterday grinding one biscuit to powder and this b------ shell does all these boxes in two seconds." All our gatherings are under cover of darkness, church parades, smoking concerts, pipe bands, etc.

The weather is fine, with occasional cold snaps, but we are now past the period when we went all day in shirt sleeves. Fancy sun-bathing in November! The traffic of war has ground the Peninsula to dust, and we are rather tormented by dust, if the wind rises above a light air, as it generally does. We are told that we may expect on the whole open and good weather till the New Year, but that then we shall be in for a very rough time. It gets very cold after sunset, and the stars shine with a brilliancy that we never see at home. It would be a fine region, if it were not for the war.

At present, however, we are speculating on the Balkan States, for their decisions and actions are of much interest to us generally. Little did any of us think a few years ago when we were reading the accounts of the Balkan wars at home in comfort that we should one day be sucked into their angry whirlpool. Yet so it has happened. It may make things better for all, but it will hasten the end.

Everybody has some vague idea of what actual war is like, but it is quite different from our imaginations. So I found, and so it has been found by everybody with whom I have compared notes. There is little romance in it. It is a disagreeable business, but we must see it through. We have only distant ideas of the actual currents of public opinion at home, but to judge from what we read in the papers there are many who do not even try to think what it all means. If they could see our soldiers hanging on desperately "in weariness and painfulness, in watchings often in hunger and thirst, in fastings often in cold and nakedness," and doing it all without a murmur, they would be so moved that they would leave all domestic disputes to one side and give the whole of their energy to see this hideous war through.

Very many thanks to you and those who have helped you in your generosity. The cigarettes have not yet turned up, but it takes three weeks for a letter, and six weeks for a parcel to reach the Peninsula. Kindest regards to Messrs Johnson & Greig personally and to any other friends. – Yours sincerely, A.J. Campbell.

Shetland Times, 15 January 1916, page 4

Anonymous. An officer of the 7th Royal Scots wrote to his relatives in Leith about the actions in the Dardanelles. The newspaper stated he was the son of Shetland parents, and was married to a Shetland lady. He was probably Captain Malcolm Smith (1885-1963), married to Margaret Sutherland, the daughter of the Shetland Sheriff Clerk, Archibald Sutherland. He was the son of the Provost of Leith, Sir Malcolm Smith (1856-1935), who was born in Hoswick. Captain Smith later won the Military Cross in Palestine.

16th November 1915

I think I told you before that we were going to attack the Turks. Well, we did so yesterday and fairly hammered them. It is difficult to describe it all; it was done so quickly, and yet it took a long time.

The ----- Rifles and ------ Yeomanry on our right and Nos. 1 and 4 Companies of ----- on our left were both to attack at 3pm. Nos. 2 and 3 Companies of the ------ were told to hold the centre of the line and give them covering fire. As we were in the firing line, we were under the ----- Rifles for orders, so Captain ----- stayed with the ----- Rifles. Lieutenant ----- had charge of the digging parties, and I had charge of the firing line, with four machine guns to increase the fire. Well, at 2.30 we all stood to arms for we thought the Turks would know we were going to attack, and try some fancy tricks. We had previously undermined the Turkish trenches, and at 3pm sharp, blew them up, Turks and all. The attacking parties dashed forward, and we opened rapid fire. What a din! rifles, machine guns, artillery, and bombs all going at once. We saw our bombers rushing along the Turkish trenches bombing the Turks out of them, and planting their blue flags to let us know where they were. It was most thrilling. Of course, we could only see a small part of the battle, for we had our own part to attend to, but the Turks seemed to be taken completely by surprise for we completely overwhelmed them right away, and it was some time before they could get their guns to bear on us. Well, to cut a long story short, the ----- Rifle and the ----- Yeomanry captured their trench and rushed the communication trenches and barricaded them and set up bomb stations. The -------th pushed on along and captured a lot of trenches. The Turks were rushed off their feet, and we carried everything before us: darkness found us going hard at it still, and in addition to the terrific din we had a terrible storm of thunder and lightning and awful rain, just solid water, so we were soaked at once, but we carried on by the glare of the rockets, star shells, and the lightning. It was terrible, and the whole scene was indescribable! Then the storm ceased and the fire began to slacken, so at 11.30pm we put the men on duty: one on and two off, to give them some sleep, and Captain ----- told me to turn in. Of course I was soaking wet and starving, so I had a hard biscuit. I couldn't go to bed for my blankets were soaking, so I just sat on my bedding in a corner, and slept like a top till 2.30am, when I woke up and relieved Captain -----.

It was fairly quiet all night, but as soon as we stood to arms at dawn, the concert began again, but with full daylight we saw that we had driven the Turks back, and were holding our new positions safely, so I took a lot of our company up to the ----- Rifles to help them to consolidate their new trench, and now I am back and dog tired.

Well, we can't have victories without losses! I don't know our exact number of causalties, but you'll be sorry to hear that poor old Flett[34] was killed. He was shot through the head three minutes after the attack began, while leading on his men to support the bombers. We are all very sorry for he was such a favourite with us all; he is the first officer of the -----th to fall in action. The ------ Rifles lost one officer, and had another wounded, and some 30 men killed and wounded.

I hope we get relieved to-morrow for this trench is in a fearful state; last night it was ankle deep in mud and water; to-day it is dry and the sun is trying to shine, so we shall get our blankets dried. I'm all dry now except my feet, but when I've time I'll change my socks, but my boots seem to be quite sodden, and I feel rheumatic twinges in my knees. We are all in such good spirits that yesterday's troubles seem quite forgotten.

Shetland News, 4 September 1915, page 4

Lance-Corporal William J. Gair (born 1893), 1/5th Highland Light Infantry, the son of William Gair, a builder, born Nesting, who had moved with his family from Lerwick to Glasgow, and Joan Anderson (then deceased). He wrote from the Dardanelles.

19 July 1915
We are back at the "rest camps" after having had five days in the support trenches, and another five in the firing line, and I can tell you it is no child's play. If ever men needed a rest it is us, owing to the lack of sleep. We came down from the firing line last night. I have lost all my equipment, including my rifle, and everything, in the glorious charge we made on the 13th instant. I am proud to say that the 5th has made a name for itself, since it came out here. We took the Brigade out of a very critical position, and our boys quite upheld the honour of the H.L.I.

There was no flinching anywhere. It was a case of "Come on boys and get it over." I can tell you I was pretty shaky before the charge; but when we lined the parapet to prepare to charge, I forgot all my nervousness in the excitement.

---

34 Probably Lieut. John Edmund Flett, Royal Scots, d. 15th November 1915

When once I got over our parapet, I thought it was all up. It was pure Hell let loose, between shrapnel and machine guns. I saw the Turks' trenches in front of me, so I said to myself, the sooner I get there the better it will be for myself. Then off I went like a streak of lightning for this trench, and I landed there without a scratch, only I got my watch smashed with a piece of shrapnel; I can tell you it was hot work; but I came through safely, thank God. Many a brave lad of the 5th and 6th H.L.I. laid down their lives for their country in that charge. If we make any more attacks like the last one, there will not be a Turk left in Turkey.

I must thank you for the parcel with the quenchers. You have no idea how much they are needed. During the last attack, I never got a drink of water or anything for twelve hours. If I am spared to get home, I will never waste another drop of water if I can help it, as long as I live.

THE NURSE

Nurse Martha Aitken in World War One.
Courtesy of Mrs P.G. Paterson.

Nurse Martha Aitken (1881-1969). On 6 February 1915 the *Shetland News* noted that Martha and Jessie Ann Aitken, daughters of the Lerwick builder Charles W. Aitken, were engaged as nurses in the war. Martha was in Boulogne, Jessie in Aberdeen. The *Daily Mail* had recently shown Martha nursing a wounded British soldier. She wrote to her parents from the 7th Casualty Clearing Station. The paper entitled the piece "Somebody's Boy." Field Marshall Haig mentioned her in despatches. In 1919 she was awarded the Royal Red Cross medal. She had an interesting life after the war, marrying and becoming Mrs Martha Withall, but was widowed shortly afterwards. She continued her nursing career in Kenya. After retirement in 1948 she visited Australia and had a short spell with the Flying Doctor service. She returned to Kenya during the Mau Mau rebellion to help a friend. She died in Edinburgh in 1969.

Shetland News, 3 April 1915, page 4

17 March 1915

Dear Mother and Father

I have a few minutes tonight to write to you. No doubt you will know we have been busy – very busy. Before the taking of Neuve Chapelle we were at work getting this place ready for the wounded, and we had a job. When I tell you one of the rooms had beds for 110, you can judge for yourself.

We heard the first shot being fired at 6 a.m. It woke me up, and I felt cold shivers running down my back. It was awful, and at each crash of the guns I thought what it meant to some poor souls. The guns boomed forth one after the other, and all together it was horrible. The noise was awful and even the ground appeared to tremble.

The enemy lost heavily, and some we had in here were very badly wounded. Some hours later the first of the wounded arrived, and we soon got them comfortable and warm. They had come straight from the field ambulance (where their wounds got the first dressing) to here, so you can picture to yourself our work. First we try to get off boots and wet clothes. Often the boots are so wet that they have to be cut off. As for uniforms they are usually stained with blood and soaking with water and mud. They are soon ripped in all directions, if the patient is not able to be moved without pain. I am afraid we have no respect for His Majesty's uniform when there is a wounded man inside it.

There are no beds, so that each man has a stretcher on the floor, but the stretchers have short legs and are made of stout canvas, so that they are quite comfortable, and the patient is not, after all, lying on the hard floor.

Socks, pyjama suits, shirts and mufflers, are always wanted, so if you know of anyone who wants to send things for the soldiers tell them to send these. If they could only see the men as I see them, they would be only too glad to do everything possible to help them.

Sometimes one would think the men had been lying in a river, they are so wet. French mud does stick, and one feels inclined to scrape it off them. Then their faces are quite yellow with the lyddite,[35] as well as the mud. It was ghastly to see them all.

Next comes the dressing of wounds. The sisters have to kneel all the time, and I can tell you that our backs and knees do ache. The men are very grateful for everything that is done for them, however little it is. It is terrible work. The men were delighted with their victory, but what a ghastly toll leads to it – a perfect inferno in one quiet village, Neuve Chapelle – bombs, guns, rifles, all banging away, and each shot claiming from one to 60 human lives.

Let us begin to look at the wounds. The first has a large shrapnel wound in the arm. The shrapnel is removed and carefully stored away as a souvenir – rather a grim one. This time it is both legs and head that are injured, and the poor man is quite unable to move. In spite of all he is very cheerful and comfortable once his wet, stained clothes are removed. It would be quite impossible to tell you about all the cases.

Half-way up the ward two boys are lying together – one a German and the other a Britisher. The former is badly wounded in the head. His continual cry is for water. He speaks broken English, and one can know he is talking of home and parents. Poor boy! After his wounds had been dressed he thanked us so gratefully. The Germans are treated in the same way as our own men. At times one does feel very bitter with them, but it is a different matter when one is laid at one's feet helpless and perhaps dying.

After all, he is somebody's boy.

Next to him is a lad shot through the chest and abdomen. He has no pain and feels very happy. His only wish is that I should write and tell his mother that he was in the famous, if terrible, battle. "Our side won, sister," he says. He would like a cup of tea like what his mother makes. I got the tea for him specially. He did enjoy it so much. He gave me his home address, and a few minutes later lay dead.

So on round the ward. Our two clergymen are a great help to us. They fetch drinks, lift and make patients comfortable, light cigarettes for the helpless, and generally cheer everybody. They even carry the stretchers to and from the ambulances.

Then comes the time when all the patients who can be moved are lifted, stretcher and all, into the ambulances and thence to the train. All get the length of one of the base hospitals, and there they get a good bed and every comfort. Once again, those who are able for another journey are sent over to England next day, and land in some hospital at home, to be nursed and cared for. The worst cases are kept here until they are able for the railway journey, and then at the base they may remain for some weeks before being sent over the Channel.

35 Lyddite – a form of high explosive.

The record in the cemetery here is known by the wooden crosses over each grave. They are many. Each one bears the name, number and regiment of the hero who has fought and fallen, and each one is buried with full military honours.

Shetland News, 29 May 1915, page 4

Extract from another letter by Nurse Martha Aitken to her parents

Just a note to say I am perfectly well and safe. All the fighting is in this direction at present, and I am sure Hell could not be worse. We are very, very busy. The men tell some ghastly tales of the cruelties of the Germans to our poor wounded and helpless men. Every man who can fight should be here to avenge the fallen. I will write when I can, but don't expect a letter as long as this lasts.

Shetland News, 5 June 1915, page 4

Nurse Martha Aitken to her parents

Outside the rain is falling in a hopeless and persistent fashion. It rattles on the corrugated iron roof, and the moaning of the wind and the clatter of windows and doors keep up a mournful accompaniment. Inside is another scene still more mournful. It is a large room full of patients with measles, and two of these very ill with pneumonia as well. The fire is cheerful, which is one comfort. Each time the door or windows shake the patients start in their sleep and moan wearily. A frightened mouse scurries across the floor and disappears in one of the many holes in the wall. The hurricane lamp by the light of which I am writing does not burn brightly; it splutters and smokes badly.

One patient is delirious, and talks and moans almost incessantly. Poor man! He is nearly always in the trenches and cannot get out except when he has to go some message. At times he talks of home. Then he rambles on about the war, and asks for assistance to pull him out of the wet, muddy trench. He sees numberless shells bursting beside him. Another time he thinks he is going on parade, and his rifle will not become clean. Sometimes it is a roll-call or a route march, and so on incessantly, – the poor fellow getting little or no sleep and losing strength all the time.

My other wards are at the other side of a large muddy square, to get to which long boots, a macintosh and a lantern are absolutely necessary in such a night as this. As I cross the square I realise that there is a great deal going on in the darkness of the night. The sound of guns and the presence of flashlights now and again does not let one forget that a terrible struggle is in progress a few miles away – the strongest machinery against the strongest machinery, and brave men behind it.

In a further letter, referred to on the same page, she wrote:

A day or two ago I watched an aeroplane duel between a British and a German machine – the latter a Taube. They were potting at each other, and so were the British and German guns from below. It was fine to see them having a fight like two great birds, and the bombs bursting all around them. Needless to say we watched with bated breath; none of us spoke, but no doubt all wished to see the German brought down. At last it was hit on the wing and came down some distance very rapidly and wobbly. However it righted itself again. This went on for a few minutes and then another British machine came in sight. That was enough for Mr German. He fled off looking rather weak and wobbly. There were several parting shots, and I think the German was hit again, but I am not sure. Our machines are splendid, and the officers are so brave and modest.

This awful gas that the Germans are using is most deadly to the men. It is worse than wounds or disease. It is awful to think that they mean to win by might. If might wins, they do; if right wins, then we do. Surely right will be right in the end.

CONDOLENCES

From the top, left to right: Row 1 Lance-Corporal M. T. Cheyne, Lance-Corporal M. Christie, Private Laurence J. Cooper; Row 2 Seaman Christopher Coutts, Trooper Edward T. Coutts, Lance-Corporal J. S. Coutts; Row 3 Private J. L. W. Erasmuson, Private George Johnston, Corporal Tom Scott; Row 4 Private. Wm. T. Spence, Sergeant Robert Williamson. No photograph of Corporal Laurence Petrie appears to survive.

Photographs: Shetland Roll of Honour and Roll of Service.

Corporal Laurence Petrie (1878-1915), 1st Scottish Horse, was born in Edinburgh, to James Andrew Petrie and Ann Gray, both from Unst. The *Shetland Times* noted he had already had a military career in the Boer War, in the Lothian and Berwickshire Yeomanry. When he was killed in the Dardanelles he left a widow and a family of five at St. David's Terrace, Edinburgh. His cousin Lance-Sergeant P.T. Petrie had been lost at Loos. His brother Edward was in France, and had taken part in the taking of Hill 70 the previous September.

Captain John Dewar, of the 6th Squadron Scottish Horse, wrote to Mrs Petrie –

I am extremely sorry to say your husband was killed here yesterday by a shell. I cannot tell you how much we feel his loss, not only because the Army loses a capable and fearless man, but because we all lose the best of friends. I have just only taken over this Squadron so have had no time to make his acquaintance for any more than a few days, but his old officers could not speak too highly of him. If it is any consolation to you in your great loss, I may tell you he suffered no pain at all and was killed instantaneously. My deepest sympathy to you and your children.

The Revd. D. Lamont, Chaplain of the Scottish Horse, also wrote to Mrs Petrie –

It is with the deepest regret and sympathy that I write to tell you that your husband Corporal Petrie (3811), 1st Scottish Horse was killed yesterday, and was buried by me last night. He was lying in his dugout when a high explosive shell came into it and killed him instantaneously. His death has been a great grief and loss to his comrades and to the officers of the regiment, as he was considered to be an excellent soldier, a good comrade, and a most excellent N.C.O. He was buried by me and Captain Dewar and two or three of his comrades at seven o'clock, the same evening, in a small burial ground for soldiers behind the trenches close to Chocolate Hill, which lies on the Salt Lake plain or Mafurtac and we laid him to his rest as reverently and tenderly as was possible a few yards from where he was killed. Captain Dewar and some other officers of his Squadron will no doubt forward you any personal possessions which he had. Nothing I can say will assuage your grief in your grievous loss but I wish to convey to you my deepest sympathy and to let you know where your husband lies as well as give you at least the comfort of knowing that he received a Christian burial. Some of his comrades told me he had left five children, and one's heart is sore for the poor bairns. May God comfort and sustain you with His fatherly hand, and abide with you and yours in your darkened home. With much sympathy.

Shetland Times, **December 9 1916, page 5**

Lance-Corporal M. Christie (1897-1916), a Gordon Highlander, was killed in France, 18 November 1916. The article said Magnus Christie had been in the grocery trade with Messrs Hall & Co., Lerwick, and was a "general favourite." He had been in the base area helping train men, and had only been ten days in the trenches before his death.

Lieut. Henderson of the Gordons wrote to his mother, Mrs Christie, Skibhoull Cottage, Cunningsburgh.

Lance-Corporal Christie, was killed on the night of the 18th November, during the recent heavy fighting in France. A piece of shell hit him, and though he was attended to at once, he died about an hour after. Lance-Corporal Christie had only been a few days with us, but had proved himself a most capable non-commissioned officer, and a cheery comrade in the trenches. Accept my deepest sympathy, and the sympathy of all the Company in your great loss. I regret that I have been unable to write you before, but the Battalion has only just returned to the trenches.

Shetland Times, **June 2 1917, page 5**

Seaman Christopher Coutts, R.N.R. (1894-1917), died of pneumonia in Chatham Naval Hospital, 9 May 1917. A nurse wrote to his mother, Robina Ann Coutts.

You will have quite realised from the last telegram that there is no chance now of his recovery. We are all so sorry you can't be with him; but the long journey would be impossible for you. At one time Christopher hoped he might get well enough to come home to you, but he has given up all thought of that now. You must comfort yourself with the knowledge that he is happy and comfortable, and in no pain. I think when the end comes, it will come very peacefully, and he will die in his sleep. He is a dear, good boy and has made himself loved by us all, and we shall miss him very much. You are a fortunate mother to have had such a good son.

Shetland Times, **December 8 1917, page 4**

Private Laurence John Cooper (1896-1917), killed in action, France, 20 November 1917. He was a Gordon Highlander, the son of Mr and Mrs John Cooper, Fleet Street, Lerwick. Lieutenant D. Peterson wrote to them.

I wish to express to you my most sincere sympathy in the loss of such a splendid son. Although I was not there at the moment he was killed, I was not far away; and I am told by the officers and non-commissioned officers who were actually there, that your son behaved most gallantly in the face of the enemy. He was a particularly smart and efficient soldier, and those who were with him that day are praising him very much indeed for his gallant conduct. Your son is buried in a cemetery, which was made on the battlefield on ground taken from the enemy.

Shetland Times, December 15 1917, page 4

Lance-Corporal A. Penny of the Gordon Highlanders also wrote a letter to Private Cooper's mother.

It was the 20th of this month (November), we were in action, and my section had to take a wood, in which the Germans were ambushed in large numbers. As we were advancing we were under very heavy rifle and machine gun fire. Laurence advanced out into the open with his Lewis gun, and started firing on the enemy, when a sniper hit him in the stomach with a bullet. He started to crawl back into a trench, when a sniper caught him in the back and killed him. He was well liked by all his comrades in the section and they all send their deepest sympathy to you in your sad bereavement.

Shetland Times, December 15 1917, page 4

Lance-Corporal J. S. Coutts (1894-1917), killed in action, 20 November 1917. John Smith Coutts, a Gordon Highlander, was the son of Captain James Coutts and his wife Wilhelmina. His mother had been widowed in 1896 and lived at 1 Pilot Lane, Lerwick. Lieutenant D. Peterson wrote to her.

I know that his platoon officer, 2nd Lieut. Duncan (who was wounded that day), had a very high opinion of your son, and often spoke to me about his great coolness and determination in action. ... Your son is buried with his chums who fell that day, in a cemetery made on the battlefield, on ground taken from the enemy.

Shetland Times, 6 July 1918, page 5.

Trooper Edward T. Coutts (1894-1917), killed in action, Egypt. Edward Thomas Jamieson Coutts was in the New Zealand Expeditionary Force, and was the eldest son of Mrs Eliza Ann Coutts, Aith, Fetlar. Trooper McKay wrote about him to a friend in New Zealand and the letter was sent home to Coutts relatives in Fetlar. The *Shetland Times* noted that the letter did not reach home in time for his mother to read it. She received news of his death, "gradually sank day after day" and died about six months later.

The writer says that Trooper Coutts died one of the bravest deaths, for he sacrificed himself for a comrade in distress. While the enemy was shelling the line, a trooper was hit by shrapnel and badly wounded. Without any thought of self, Trooper Coutts went to his assistance, and stood out in the open dressing his wounds, when a shell came over and killed him instantly. Had he looked to himself and sought cover, the chances are he would have been alive yet. He was one of the crew of a Hotchkiss gun, and had played his part in dealing with the enemy before he "went under." He was a genial, good hearted lad, and was very popular with his mates, all of whom agreed that he had met a hero's death.

Shetland Times, August 24 1918, page 5

Corporal Tom Scott (1890-1918), Australian Light Horse. Thomas Moffat Scott was killed action, serving in Palestine. He was the son of Captain John Scott of the s.s. *St Rognvald*. Lieut. A.S. Goodchild wrote to his father.

Dear Captain Scott, – You have, no doubt, been informed ere this of the death of your son, Corporal T. M. Scott. I was his troop leader, and as such write to tell you that Tom was an excellent soldier and a gentlemanly fellow, who stood a good chance of getting a commission, so that you may derive some small comfort from the knowledge that he lived his life with credit to himself and parents. He was a section leader, and called his men "Walids" (i.e. Arabic for boys), and they would do anything for him. "Bally," as he was nick-named, and his "Walids" were quite a well-known and bright feature of the squadron.

On the morning of his death, our line was broken by Germans in the Jordan Valley, 10 miles north of Jericho, and we were rushed in to attack them. We drove them back and occupied their position, but were heavily shelled. We had six men killed outright, among whom was your son. He is buried where he fell – 10 miles north of Jericho.

Allow me to express my deepest sympathy with you and Mrs Scott in your great loss. – Yours sincerely, A. S. Goodchild, Lieut.

D. McBean, a trooper in Corporal Scott's unit, also wrote:

Dear Sir, – It is my painful duty to write you on behalf of myself and comrades in "A" squadron, to express sincere sympathy with you in the loss of a good son and a great soldier. We all regret the loss sustained by you, our loss of a good comrade, and the nation's loss of a man. He died at his post, and fills a soldier's grave at the "Bluff" Jericho plains, the scene of a great victory for Great Britain, which he did his share to bring about. He gave his life for his country. His gain; our loss. On behalf of his sorrowing comrades. – Yours Sincerely, D. McBean, Trooper.

Shetland Times, September 21 1918, page 5

Private James Laurence W. Erasmuson (1895-1918). Killed in action, France, 4 September 1918. He was in the Machine Gun Guards, the son of Mr and Mrs William Erasmuson, 9 Chromate Lane, Lerwick. Major F. Talberts wrote to his mother.

It is with very real sorrow that I write to tell you that your son was killed instantaneously without pain on 4th September. He was buried by some of his friends and a cross is put over him, and a service read by the grave. You will hear from the Guard Registration Commissioner where he was buried. It may be some comfort to you to know that he was killed during a big advance, and that the Germans are never likely to recapture the ground where he lies. You have the deepest sympathy of us all – officers and men – in your great loss. Your son would have been a great help in reorganising the company had he lived. Since he is dead we cannot do more than think of him and wish him well.

Lieutenant C. W. Duncan wrote to Mrs Erasmuson:

Dear Madam – I regret that the subject of my letter to you is one which will cause you much pain and sorrow. We all out here run almost daily risks and some are luckier than others. I most sincerely regret to have to tell you that your son, Private J. Erasmuson, was killed on September 4th about 1 p.m. in the afternoon, by a shell landing straight on the shelter where he was living. I fully realise that any words of mine can do but little to alleviate your great loss, but I would like to express to you the thorough trust and confidence which I have always been able to place in your son. He has been under my personal command ever since he came to France, and in the time that elapsed since then I have always found him a keen soldier, most conscientious, and more trustworthy than most. He was ever popular in his section and his cheerfulness under often most trying circumstances helped many. We did all that was possible under the circumstances afterwards: He was buried on the western side of Louverval Wood, after a full service had been conducted and he lies close to the place where he fell, and next to him lies Corporal Crock, who fell from the "same shell." I feel sure that you may be relieved to hear that he did not suffer at all but that death claimed him instantaneously. May I once more express my most sincere sympathy with you at your sad bereavement and should you at any time wish for any further particulars, if you will let me know I shall only be too pleased to do all that if possible.

Shetland Times, September 28 1918, page 4

Private William T. Spence (1892-1918) was killed in action, France, 21 August 1918. William Thomas Spence was in the Gordon Highlanders, and was the son of the late Mr Andrew Spence and Mrs Spence, Cullivoe, Yell. The Chaplain wrote to Mrs Spence.

Dear Mrs Spence, – I am very sorry to have to inform you of the death of your son, Pte. Wm. Spence, who was killed last week end in the course of the present fighting. He was killed instantaneously, and this I hope may bring you some small measure of comfort in your great sorrow. There is little which a stranger can say which may console you. This brings the war so grievously home to you and I wish to assure you of our sorrow and sympathy and to acquaint you of the fact that by your son's death the battalion has lost a good soldier, faithful and efficient in the discharge of his duty, and we all have lost a true comrade, whom we felt would stand by us in the time of need. So today we regard him with a proud and grateful, if sorrowful, memory.

Shetland Times, 28 September 1918, page 4

Sergt. Robert Williamson (1870-1918). Killed in action, France, 2 September 1918. He was an Artificer Sergeant, Australian Field Artillery, the son of Mr and Mrs Andrew Williamson, High Street, Lerwick. He had served in the Boer War. He had been wounded at Gallipoli and later in France. The Chaplain wrote to Sergt. Williamson's mother.

By the time this reaches you, you will probably have received official notification of the death of No. 1893, Sergt. R. Williamson, Australian Field Artillery, which occurred on 2nd instant. I write as Chaplain of the Brigade to convey to you the sympathy of the Colonel, officers, N.C.O.'s and men at the loss of so fine a son. He was a fine man, a brave soldier, popular and respected by all ranks. That your grief at his loss may be alleviated by the knowledge that he did his duty to the Empire, and died in a great cause, and that the consolation of Divine grace may be a real experience in these dark hours, is my prayer for you. ... We buried him on the morning of September 4, in the British Military Cemetery at Clery. The Battery erected a cross at his head as a tribute to his memory. Will you please accept my own personal sympathy at the loss of a man whom I have learned to esteem very highly.

Shetland Times, 5 October 1918, page 5

Lance-Corporal M. T. Cheyne (1896-1918), Gordon Highlanders, was killed in action, France, 20 July 1918. He was Malcolm Thomas Cheyne, son of Mr and Mrs Sinclair Cheyne, Ireland, Bigton. His Company Officer wrote to Mrs Cheyne.

I very much regret to inform you of the death of your son ... who was killed in action on the 20th July, while gallantly doing his duty. I knew that he was slightly wounded about the ear, earlier in the day, and had been back at the doctor to have it dressed, returning again to the firing line at his own request. Later in the day, he was hit by fragments of a shell, and lived barely an hour. He was buried on the Battlefield near where he was hit.

I had known him since the winter of 1914-1915, and feel his death very keenly. His platoon officer (who I regret to say, was also killed a day or two later) had a very high opinion of your son's abilities as a non-commissioned officer, and had told me that he meant to have him promoted again at an early date.

Our Chaplain is also writing to you, and the other officers of the battalion join me in sincere sympathy with you.

Private George Johnston (1893-1918). Killed in action, France, 30 August 1918. He was in the Gordon Highlanders, son of Mr and Mrs George Johnston, Tresta, Aithsting. The Chaplain of the Battalion wrote to Mrs Johnston.

I am very sorry to have to inform you of the death of your son, who was killed on the 30th August, in the course of our present advance. He was killed instantaneously. You are called on to bear a great grief. ... Death is so very busy and sorrow is so common. We are sorrowing with you on our own account, as well as on yours, for your son was much to us too. He had a good name in the Battalion, well he earned it, and worthily he kept it. He was devoted to, and active and eager in, the discharge of his duty. He had the spirit of good comradeship and of helpful friendship, so our Battalion has lost a good soldier, and friends have lost a good comrade, and in our own feeling of loss we sympathise with you in your loss, which is much greater.

Robert Jamieson

Robert Jamieson (1890-1918), was the son of James Jamieson and Barbara Ann Williamson, Lerwick. He was a bright, engaged, politically active member of the community (an adherent of Hyndman's British Socialist Party), working in John Brown's business at Freefield. His brother Peter, who was very fond of him, preserved his letters. The letters to his family at 21 St Magnus Street, Lerwick, are upbeat, perhaps consciously so, full of humour and Shetland dialect. He appreciated the new things he saw, especially France, but died there of wounds on an ambulance train. His initial letters were from the training establishment at Cromarty. The letters are mostly addressed to Peter Jamieson, and his brother Jim [Jeamsie], and there are references to their sister Margaret in Edinburgh.

Shetland Archives D9/410/44/9

16th July 1917

Dear Mam,

... I have just come down from Ord Pinders Circus. They are here for one night. They are the same circus folk that used to visit poor old Lerrick years ago. Their big tent & Circus is just up in our parade ground whar I used to drill. Poor body am doing nae dreel eenoo a less da auld bayonet fighting of a hunder years back. Dat il no kill mony Germans. We have an hours practice at it every night for wir fine show we are haddin in Alness.

Shetland Archives D9/410/44/10

24 July 1917

Dear Mother,

... There is another Shetlander in signalling class with me. A young chap, Sammy Gray, son of Hunter Gray who works for J. W. Robertson. ... I see the herring are a fine price in Lerwick according to the South papers. 3d a piece. Weel dat's a price.

Shetland Archives D9/410/44/11

31st July 1917

Dear Pete,

... Out practising sending & reading the flags & reading the electric lamp & <u>begbie</u> lamp which is a lamp they use in the daytime. It is great fun sitting up in the fields on your backside reading the dots & dashes from lamp about ½ a mile away. We sit in pairs. ... Then we also have a new business, called the Louvre Disc (a French get up) on which is made dots & dashes, that we read & write down time aboot. Then we got Flag reading (the easiest of the lot) altho' none of it is hard to pick up. In the forenoons we sit inside reading the buzzar.[36] The buzzar is an Electric battery that we make dots and dashes on. Each one gets his turn to send to the rest of the class (great fun). It is the same instrument as in Post Offices at the end of Telegraph wires or Cables & it is very easy to read at least I like it all right and have no trouble to read or send from it. It is what chiefly is used in France connecting one dug-out with another, where the signaller can sit in safety reading & writing.

... The Germans getting pretty nervous about America's preparations & dey are trying to start peace negotiations (or intrigue rather) among all the neutrals. ...

Shetland Archives D9/410/44/13

14 August 1917

Dear Peter,

Is there any word at all from Bobbie or Magnie Johnson noo a' days? Yes Artie Nicolson & Jock Newlands are home just now on draft leave. They should have been back now but Shetland is Shetland still & I warn de'll no be in a hurry.

Peter Greig's (the famous Peter of "Current Topics") son[37] is here now in hut 90. He came here last week from Blackpool. He was in the RAMC, but there is some upturn among them now. They are sending their fit men out off it & filling their places with B1 & C1 men and that sort of thing. He has been in them over a year. So he chose the Seaforths and was bundled up to Cromarty. Bobbie is his name and a nice chap he is.

Well we had a great day at Alness on Saturday. We went over to Invergordon in the morning with a drifter. Took the train for Alness & marched to Dalmore Park (fine park laid out for the occasion with tents, shows, racing grounds, band stands and so on. ... There was a great crowd of folks. The Black Watch from Nigg, the Camerons from Invergordon & of course the Seaforths from Cromarty were there and some Americans! & Canadians too. There was tugs of war, running, high jumping & what not. We gave our exhibition of the ancient bayonet fighting in the afternoon before many spectators who cheered us greatly! The Old Colonel was so pleased with us of the bayonet team, that he had us specially paraded before him last night to thank us! Poor body he's no ill ta plase. However we

---

36 Buzzar. Probably the "buzzer" a combined telegraph/telephone device used where lines were poor.

37 Robert Greig (1891-1938), *Shetland Times* journalist. A book of his writing about his war experience, *Doing His Bit*, was published in 1999. Current Topics was a column in the *Shetland Times* written by his father, Peter.

spent a most enjoyable day on Saturday & never returned back to camp till nearly midnight. No less a person than a <u>Sir</u> somebody Pears rear-Admiral[38] opened the performance and a <u>Sir</u> Hector Monroe was also there.

Shetland Archives D9/410/44/14

Tuesday 28th August 1917

Dear Peter,

... I have got up among the signallers now. Up to E. Coy, Hut 72. ... The boys were showing the Sergeant my sketchbook last night & he was delighted with it. ...

... There is a sergeant here who is going to take the photo of our bayonet team some of this fine nights. ...

Shetland Archives D9/410/44/15

5th Sept 1917

Dear Peter,

... What tinks do I wis at the head of the class. I had 100 marks for reading the buzzar. 100 marks for reading the lamp, 99 for the flag & 99 for reading the "Louvre disc." So I had an average of 99 ½ marks. ...The Sergeant was in the other night with 2 packets of Gold Flake to me for being top of the class! ...

Shetland Archives D9/410/44/16

Tuesday 25th Sept. 1917

Dear Jeamsie,

... Well there is another Lerwick chap who came here last week, Donny Gunn, "wir" peerie Lizzie's lad it we used to see in Blacks back do minds. He is a Lance Corporal ... he was out 4 months in France & got gassed but he is looking none the worse & feeling all right. He was home in Lerwick for 10 days leave from hospital & came back here to Cromarty. I had a letter yesterday from Artie Nicolson fae France. He has got into the Labour Company & likes it fine. He says Jock Newlands was sent straight to Hospital when he come out there. He had a sore leg that a horse once kicked so they bundled him to hospital!

38 Probably Rear Admiral Sir Edmund Radcliffe Pears (1862-1941)

Shetland Archives D9/410/44/17

Sunday 30th Sept. 1917

Dear Pete

... Boy we had a great concert here last night given by the officers, that Gunn & me was at ... the best was a reproduction of Bairnsfather's[39] play "Old Bill & Co". It was well carried out by the officers.

They were sitting in regular well got up dug-outs on the stage & smoke & fire & bangs representing big guns were going off behind them & shells & grenades flying about & it was very realistic & all the time Old Bill & our Bert & Alf were joking in good Bairnsfather style.

Yes there wid a been some stir among da ald weemen whin da Balloons came, Lerrick is aye blyde o' some kind o' excitement.

Shetland Archives D9/410/44/18

Monday 8th Oct 1917

Dear Pete

... Well da next bit a dye letter is about dis "blooming war" & hoping it will be ower afore Xmas Weel hit mite be for dere doeing bra weel da noo. But just tak my plan & tak every day is he comes & never bother aboot da morn & dey will surely get tired o' feeghting sometime. So even J. D. Ratter has to go. Dey canna be many in LK. [Lerwick] noo a days.

... I ca hit extravagance to write on one side o' da paper only the wye it do does. So tak dat. ...

Shetland Archives D9/410/44/19

Tuesday 26th October 1917

Dear Jim,

... All the signallers have been put into this nice new hut (83 & 84) now that the cold days have come.

... I am always sent in charge of a group. We go away up the fields & signal to another group & that group signals to another group & so on. It is mostly all young English boys so we have great times. Then we have telephones. We lay the wires from the top of the parade ground all along the top of the field to another field & signal through the 'phone & then these messages are sent by the flags all over the places where the groups are, so we waste the whole afternoon over it.

We had a great concert here in the Y.M. Hut again on Saturday. Part two of "Old Bill & Coy" (Bairnsfather's) was given & we had some good laughs at it. It

---

39 Bruce Bairnsfather (1887-1959), a humorist and cartoonist of World War One. Famous for the character "Old Bill."

was even funnier than Part one. Another good thing at the concert was a band competition between the different "Coys." Each Coy got up a comic band & each performed after the other & 4 officers were the judges & the signallers band took the first prize (they got no less than £2. 10/- for the first prize which was jolly good divided among 7 of them (I wish I could play like dee and I sood a been in the band.)

Shetland Archives D9/410/44/19

Sunday 28th October 1917

Dear Jim,

... We had an exam last week and I had the highest possible marks 100 in each subject making an average of 100. So I again carried off the fags. We are getting our final exam this week "the Brigade Test" as they call it & if I do as well in that I will carry off the cross flags ... a photo we my left airm decorated we twa cross flags wid be mare worth sending.

Dis is Sunday we wis & we're just come fae da Kirk – we go every Sunday morning at 9.30 am & dan da rest o' da day is wir aen.

Shetland Archives D9/410/44/19

Tuesday 6th Nov 1917

Dear Jim,

You are still lamenting aboot da war well I warn, but as long as I get my cross flags am no just very particular aboot da war for I will get a good job safe & comfortable in France or anywhere. They call the signallers the "big lasses" because it's an easy safe job but that's just spite because it needs brains & smartness which every soldier hasn't got! What tinks do.

So Lowrie is going tae join da colours well dey canna be mony left in Lerrick noo a' days aless Admirals & the big boodies. So 21 is got a box for da brushes! ... And the sugar tickets. Well you're getting on.

Shetland Archives D9/410/44/24

Friday 21st December 1917

Dear Jim

... We are having a great Xmas concert here tonight. ... Freddie Leask is here now & a Murray boy "My rehearsal" nephew and the Peterson boy that was in Kays. ... So dir a gaddering o' Shetlanders here now.

... (This is the da year the Americans is going to finish its war if Kaiser Bill's Xmas Peace terms are not accepted by the Allies!) So ony wye dey like noo I am got my lst class certificate!

Shetland Archives D9/410/44/25

Replying after receiving a telegram worrying about not hearing from him due to delay in his letter arriving.

Thursday 27th Dec 17.

Dear Pete,

... So if there is any delay in the letters you will have to take the Irishman's plan (which is also my own): the Irishman said "if you canna be aisy be as aisy as you can". ... I was at the Doctor (known as the "plumber" in the army) today & he was not ower weel pleased at my heart! (which does not bother me however) & I also spun him a yarn aboot varicose veins in my right leg (another thing which does not bother me, but of course I didn't tell him that) so if I go he is going to recommend ... me for a base job! Good old boy!

I am going to take not "ma peerie testament" as "Kirkhouse Johnny" wid say ... but "ma peerie sketch book." It will be great getting sketches of France!

... So I will likely be for France very soon but I am not troubling myself in the least. ... Well 1918 is coming & the war will no last more than six months at the very very longest, and thats only 24 weeks & do noos how fast a week can go, so cheer up for I am in the best of spirits after my visit to the "plumber".

... Meg was also saying that P. Jamieson was home from France for a fortnight's leave. Thats another good thing about France you get more than a weeks leave at a time.

... We had a great day here on Xmas. It was a whole holiday we wis & we got a great breakfast & fancy dinner & tea.

Shetland Archives D9/410/5

Written on a coloured Celesque Letter Card with five views of Folkstone.

11 a.m, 4th Jan 1918.

Folkestone

Dear Jim,

... arrived in London at 4.30 this morning after having a grand 24 hours trip in the train. We were in the same carriage all the way from Cromarty to London & didn't have to bother shifting our train.

... And man hit's wirt joining the army for to see the splendid country known as Great Britain. The scenery & views are great & as for London! weel, aall hadd me tongue! ... We are all staying in a big fancy hotel! We cross over to Calais in the afternoon. The only signs I've seen yet o' dis great war is wan lonely airoplane hovering high in the clouds over this lovely place but it is an English one! ... Tons of soldiers here coming & going to the seat o' da great waar.

Shetland Archives D9/410/44/27

21507 Sig. R. Jamieson
Seaforths
In Scottish Base Depot
c/o A.P.O., S/24 B.E.F.
France

Sunday 6th Janry 1918

Mon cher frere Jacques,

Now there's a start off, that's the way I "parlee" here to the French folk. ...
    ... This is Sunday with us so we are just visiting the Y.M.C.A.'s for a "bun scoff" & tea & the pictures every night & strolling about seeing this lovely country with its wonderful buildings & sights.
    Eh bien, je serais fini pour cette temps avec les plus meillieur regards aux toutes les familles des votre frère Robbe.

Shetland Archives D9/410/44/28

21057 Sig. R. Jamieson, Seaforths
M Scottish Base Depot
C/O A.P.O., S/24, B.E.F.
France

Thursday 10th Jan. 1918

Mon cher frere Pierre,
... We go visiting the cafes where we get splendid meals very cheap when we want them. The grub in camp is excellent & plenty of it & good billets & we get a bath when ever we feel inclined so I see nought to grumble at.
    We have good pictures & concerts every night. There is a big Y.M. here & Salvation Army Hall & Scottish Churches Hut & so on where we get splendid tea & have a "bun scoff" noo in dan. In fact, I think, eating is the most we do! Lang may it lest. You should hear me parleying to the French boys & women who come round the camp selling chocolate & apples!
    We deal in French money here & great fun getting into the swing of it.

Shetland Archives D9/410/44/29

21057 Sig. R. Jamieson, Seaforths
M Scottish Base Depot
C/O A.P.O., S/24, B.E.F.
France

Sunday 13th Jan 1918

Dear Jim

... Altho' it's called France, it's the best place I have been in yet & I am enjoying myself here better than anywhere yet. I wish you could see it!

... Enclosed is an envelope addressed as it should be, as the base may be shifted anytime & then it will likely be forwarded.

Shetland Archives D9/410/44/30

21057 Sig. R. Jamieson, Seaforths
M Scottish Base Depot
C/O A.P.O., S/24, B.E.F.
France
Wednesday 16th Jan. 1918

Mon cher frere Pierre,

... We have very good concerts & pictures here. On Monday night we had a special actress singing & playing for us in the Y. M. Hall. We also had free tea, chocolate, matches, Buns & "Fags" in the "Scottish Churches' Hut" on Monday. So we are having great times!

... I saw Tommy White yesterday passing the Depot on his way "up the line", & a Thomson boy who used to be in Stove & Smith's.

Shetland Archives D9/410/44/31

[Address blacked out]
France

Saturday 19th January 1918

Dear Pete,

... For this is a fine country to be in - Better weather & better times than in "Blighty."

This is Saturday night & I am scrawling this in the Y.M. while the piano is drumming ahead & the boys are singing & tea drinking & "bun-scoffing" as usual. "That's the stuff to give the troops" as they say in the Army. Some life this! It's the most enjoyable I have ever had anyhow. So many nice chaps & interesting sights. A sketch-book comes in handy here, or rather would come if you had the chance to use it.

We came here to this nice quiet little place yesterday from the last bigger place, so I am seeing quite a lot of this interesting country - France. I am still doing next to nothing. Well I am eating & drinking & smoking "tons" of this "fags" here which are very cheap in this quarter. We also get a free issue of fags so we're no "ill aff."

I may tell you we are in nice huts with a fire here & it is a great improvement to the last big place - where we were "under canvas." Altho' I agreed well with tents (having once stayed in "Soond") some of the boys grumbled at it. But they never knew the joys of "camping out" like me as I told them, for tents are very cosy & comfortable here as the weather is much milder & better than in "Blighty." Anyhow we have splendid huts here & good times.

Shetland Archives D9/410/44/32

21057 Sig. R. Jamieson
1 Coy., 1 Platoon,
4th Seaforths,
B.E.F. France
6.30 p.m. Tuesday
22nd Jan. 1918

Dear Pete,
Just a line to show you another address! So many millions of men here. I suppose that you must be well detailed to "distinguish" one from the "tother" ... so don't be surprised at the continual changing of address.

... I am in the pink & enjoying myself "tip top." I wish you could see this interesting country. I may tell you am at another place from that which I wrote the last letter (if you have got it!). This place is the best yet. In tents at the first place, huts last place, & here we are billeted in splendid private houses. So "hit's aye goed it betters". Anyhow "thats the stuff to give the troops," good accommodation like this & the grub is excellent both in quantity & quality & fags galore, not to mention the "tot of rum" every night for every man who wants it, & why refuse what's going? Not me.

I am writing this in the Y.M. here (Y.M's wherever one goes in this country). My nice English signalling chum is also busy writing alongside me replying to letters which he has only got tonight from Derby England. Some of them wrote over a month ago, so no wonder I am not looking for any letters from the far North for a few days yet.

... So I think we have got a permanent address this time so I'll be hearing "fae ye" sometime. Whether you believe me or no I am <u>not</u> wearying for word yet & neither "wid do" if "do wis" training about from one town or village to another in this interesting country. I hope I have made "de teeth water" by this time, laying it on thick about the interest of this place. But it's a fact. I will be forced to use my sketch book in this lovely little village we are now in.

... Well as I was saying we went away "umpteen kilometres" from the last village, we were in, for a walk in the afternoon, & visited the old front line which was evacuated (in the north of France) last year about Feb, or March! How would do like to have been with us & seen the trenches, dug-outs & what not of interest

& farther I will not say [more] for fear of Mr Censor's blue pencil, but we had an excellent sight & spent an excellent day.

Well we arrived here yesterday the 21st lucky number that & I am starting with the signalling section at Hqrs tomorrow morning. So that's tres bon. The weather here is really good & I am having grand times.

Excuse these poverty looking things "Field-Post Cards" if you get any as they are handy to slip in the P.O. when I am too lazy to write.

Well I will finish meantime. Hoping all are in their usual

from Robt Jamieson

Shetland Archives D9/410/44/34

21057 Sig. R. Jamieson
SignalSection
4th Seaforths
B.E.F. France
Monday 28.1.18

Dear Pete,
Just to show you another address! ... I had another letter from Meg on Saturday. It was written on Sunday the 13th! So the "Blighty" letters have started. It only took a fortnight to travel, so that's not bad! Is it?

... I am staying in a room with only 4 other boys so we are having grand times & thoroughly enjoying ourselves. "Working" only in the forenoons & having all afternoon to ourselves to go visiting from one lovely village to another & so on. The weather here is really excellent. Just like summer this last week. Fine bright sunshine every day, so I am quite enjoying my "Continental" tour & am "in the pink" of health & the very best of spirits (rum at night!) So as a L.K. boy once said "News is as scarce as coo's dung in the 'Auld Kirk'". I'll close this very very short note with best respects & all the rest of it to all the members of the Royal Family of 21 from Robt. Jamieson

Shetland Archives D9/410/44/37

21057 Sig. R. Jamieson,
SignalSection,
4th Seaforths,
B.E.F.
France

Tuesday 11.2.18

Dear Pete,
... I have had 3 from Meg, before receiving your ones, but Edina is not Thule & then again has not my address undergone some "lightning revolutions," since I started my Continental tour? ... That's but 6 or 7 yours of the 3rd has taken.

Quick work after all! No it's not so much the strictness of the Censor (re yours of Jan 28th) as my trying to be too "explicate". Some snow you must have had, but the weather here is as "Auld Airty" wid say "very necessitous baith for the fighting & so for the troops." Sorry I can't "lapse" into "Shetland" when I feel inclined. So yon wee bit will be enough for Mr Blue Pencil to worry over! Good luck to Johnson if the snow kept him a bit longer. The 'Brilliant' has gone, well we must be winning & only a few trawlers left. What are they going to do in old L.K. now? You "don't suppose the war will last much longer now" say you. Well I don't know, all I say nowadays is "Ask America!" & is not the spring coming? So "carry on".

... Mac Mouat must have forgot himself. Is there no word from him yet? Willie will be delighted to "set sail" for W. Africa for you have no idea how the Scandinavian blood asserts itself once you begin to tour round. Anyhow I am not sorry, but jolly glad I started voyaging to these interesting parts. We had a splendid concert on Saturday night & last night (tho' Sunday) I was at the Theatre & real good it was..... Yes there is always some "Old Rockers" about. Tommy Pottinger (who used to be in Black's) is a Lance Cpl. in one of our Companys! I knew I would make "de" teeth water & I am sure you'd like to see this interesting country where you can see Indians, Chinese & what not. So Meg has decided to come home in the summer as Jeamie says "she's said that before." But time will tell. Sorry my "French" was of the common or garden sort for Mr Censor but having no text books I couldn't be too "technical." However it works all right when spoken if not written.

Shetland Archives D9/410/44/38

21057 Sig. R. Jamieson,
Signal Section, 4th Seaforths, B.E.F. France

Saturday 16.2.18

This not being censored or sent off till tomorrow explains the 17.2.18 on back of envelope to give you an idea how long it 'travels' from Flanders to the "Old Rock" as Willie would call it. I wonder if he will "set up" the "BLUE CLOD' in the wilds of Africa? R.J. [Written sideways at top of letter.]

Dear Jim,
"Just one line to show you" I'm in the best of health & spirits & having good times & enjoying myself, "très bon."

I had a letter from Meg yesterday ... She was telling me she had been to a lecture on the War (that's the Great WAR, I suppose it's still going on?) Is it? Tho' the Daily papers are knocking about here, I rarely read them, as the interesting countryside claims most of my 'tention [attention]. Well let's get back to my story after that digression! You will see I am always fond of 'digressions' or extenuations rather.

... She was saying the Lecturer didn't know if the war would be over this year or not, but one thing was certain we were beating the Huns! Too true. Says I to her (I'm afraid she doesn't get too much satisfaction oot o' me) ... "No I don't suppose your lecturer or any other knows when it will be over but they're all fond of prophesying. However it won't last so long as it has lasted & will be over when it's finished!" Somewhat Irish is it not? Anyhow it'll do Marget ower weel.

"... The weather is still very 'necessitous,' both for the visiting & sae for the trips" (thro' Flanders).

... "News" is very limited & this is quite enough for 'Mr "Reademall."

With best respects to the "Old Folks" & all of 21 & the same to yersell from votre frere Robt. J.

Shetland Archives D9/410/44/39

Sig. R. Jamieson 21507,
SignalSection, 4th Seaforths, B.E.F. France

Friday 22.2.18

Dear Jack, Sam & Pete![40]
Tut! Tut! what am I saying or writing rather. <u>No</u> never mind the first two, pay "'tention" to the last. Oh but has not Jack done well & is not Sam (thats old uncle Sam) hurrying up to strafe "dem" Huns. Well I'll have to <u>commence</u> & <u>start</u> at the <u>beginning</u> again, so here goes.

Dear "Pete" Just <u>a</u> line ... of course one can't put down all one would like as Mr "Lookemallover" has to be considered. Not that I have any complaint to make – far from it, but I'd like to tell you more about things in general. ...

... let's get back to where I was. The which I was going to say (referring to the weather) is very convenient for us "Tommies" & enables us to go all over 'them' interesting parts & view the scenes of the "Greatest War in History!"

How'd you like to accompany us & see such places as inspired Bairnsfather to his flights of humour & "art" some sights! Eh?

Hoping all of "21" are in their same old way. To whom give my best respects & same 2 U from votre frère
R. Jamieson

---

40 "Jack, Sam, and Pete – a reference to the stories about three adventurers in the Boys' Friend Library.

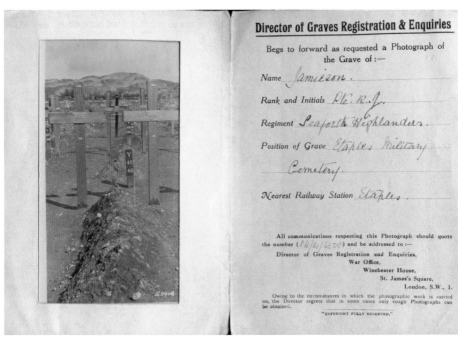

Robert Jamieson's grave. Shetland Archives, Peter Jamieson Collection, D9/411/2.

Index

Abd el Kheir, 39

Abdel Baigi, 38

Aberdeen, 62

Abiad, 37

Abrolhos Island, 46

Abu Zereiga, 38

Active, H.M.W., 50

Africa, 34, 84

Africa, effects of living in, 41, 42

Aircraft, 25, 37, 47, 65, 79

Aith, Fetlar, 69

Aitken, Charles W., 62

Aitken, Jessie Ann, 62

Aitken, Martha, 61-65

Aitken, Tammy, 26

Algiers, 53

Allison, Arthur W., 12

Allison, Capt. George and Barbara, 12

Alness, 74, 75

Ambulance, 24, 62, 63, 69, 74

Anderson, Francis, 54

Anderson, Joan, 59

Andre, River, 32

Anonymous, 19, 52, 58

Arabs, 36, 38, 39

Army Service Corps, 19

Arras, 22, 28

Australian Forces, 21, 55, 56, 70, 72

Bairnsfather, Bruce, 77, 85

Balkans, 57

Barbed wire, 14, 16, 17, 24, 25

Bayonets, 12, 21, 23, 25, 31, 56, 74-76

Begbie Lamp (signalling), 74

Belgium, 45

Big Rab, 9

Binyon, Laurence (poet), 29

Bir Watain, 38

Black Watch, 75

Blance, Jamie, 28

Blance, Jane, 14

Blatchford, Robert, 29, 30

Blatchford, Winifred, 30

Blighty, 28, 81-83

Boer War, 67, 72

Bombs (aerial), 37

Bombs (see grenades)

Boulogne, 24

Brazil, 45

Breslau, S.M.S., 35

Bristol, H.M.S., 46

British Socialist Party, 74

Brook War Hospital, 22

Brown, Andrew, 46

Brown, James, 9, 15

Burgh Road, Lerwick, 26

Burra Isle, 24

Buzzar (signal equipment), 75, 76

Bylands, s.s., 10

Byrne, Andrew, 14

Byrne, Andrew Leith Hay, 14

Calais, 13, 79

Calcutta, 10

Cameronians (see Scottish Rifles), 75

Campbell, Alexander, 32

Campbell, Alexander snr., 32

Campbell, Miss J.J., 26

Campbell, Revd. A.J., 56, 58

Camel Corps, 37, 38-40

Canadian Forces, 21, 21, 24, 25, 75

Cannell, Frank Inglis, 13, 14

Cannell, Revd. William Morrison and
Agnes, 13, 14

Cap Trafalgar, S.M.S., 45, 46

Carmania, H.M.S., 45, 46

Castle, Major, 37

Caudry, 9

Cemeteries, 64, 69, 72

Censor, 45, 83, 84, 85

Channel, English, 63

Charlottenburg, 48

Chatham Naval Hospital, 68

Cheyne, Malcolm Thomas, 66, 72

Cheyne, Sinclair, 66, 72

Chind, 37

Chinese, 50, 51, 84

Chocolate Hill, 67

Christie, Magnus, 68

Chromate Lane, Lerwick, 70

Church Lane, Lerwick, 19

Cigarettes and tobacco, 8, 9, 12, 15,
31, 32, 38, 57, 58, 63, 76, 78, 81, 82

Clarion newspaper, 29-32

Clery, 72

Coal box (shell), 13

Cooper, John, 68

Cooper, Laurence J., 68

Corkish, William H., 45

Cornwall, H.M.S., 46

Coulson, Leslie (poet), 26, 28

Coutts, Christopher, 68

Coutts, Edward Thomas Jamieson,
66, 69

Coutts, Eliza Ann, 69

Coutts, James, 69

Coutts, John Smith, 66, 69

Coutts, Robina Ann, 68

Coutts, Wilhelmina, 69

Cromarty, 29, 74-76, 79

Cunningsburgh, 17, 68

Dalmore Park, 75
Dardanelles, 56-59, 67
Darfur, 36, 40
Devon, 52
Dewar, John, 67
Dibbis, 37-39
Dinar, Ali, 36-41
Dongalawi (tribe), 39
Duncan, Lieut. C.W., 71
Duthie, Bert, 51

Egypt, 69
Egyptian Army, 36
El Fasher, 37, 38, 40
El Obeid, 36
Erasmuson, J.L.W., 66, 70
Erasmuson, William, 70
Euphorbia, s.s., 47, 53
Evans, Colonel H.C., 44
Exmouth, H.M.S., 45

Fadl, Mahommed, 39, 40
Fairview, Gulberwick, 16
Falklands, Battle of, 46, 47
Fire weapons, 14
Fish tails (mortar), 20
Fladdabister, 17
Flanders, 84, 85
Fleet Street, Lerwick, 68
Flett, John Edmund, 59
Folkestone, 79
Fort Charlotte, 44
Freefield, Lerwick, 74

French, Field Marshall, 10
Frostmann, Walter, 53
Fual el naga, 38
Fur (tribe), 39
Furowia, 43

Gair, William, 59
Gair, William J., 59
Gallipoli, 55-60, 72
Garrick, Arthur Thomas, 24
Garrick, Peter, 24
Gas, poison, 12, 13, 19, 25, 65, 76
Gibraltar, 35
Girlsta, 10, 47
Glasgow, 59
Glasgow, H.M.S., 47
Glengyle, s.s., 50
Glenfield, Dunrossness, 56
Goeben, S.M.S., 35
Goodchild, Lieut. A.S., 70
Gordon Highlanders, 9, 10, 15, 16, 28,
    68, 69, 71, 72, 73, 75
Grave, 29, 48, 64, 70, 71, 86
Gray, Ann, 67
Gray, David, 11
Gray, Hunter, 74
Gray, Ogilvy and Helen, 11
Gray, Sammy, 74
Graylingwell War Hospital, 11
Greig, Peter, 75
Greig, Robert, 75
Grenades, 17, 19, 21, 20, 25, 77, 58,
    59, 63
Groningen, 49
Groves, Major, 37

Gunn, Angus, 18
Gunn, Donny, 76
Gunn, Robert Rose, 18

Haig, Field Marshall, 62
Harbour Street, Lerwick, 44
Hardy, Charles, 47, 53
Hardy, David, 10
Hardy, Janet, 47
Hardy, Thomas, 10, 47
Henderson, Ann, 50
Henderson, Lieut., 68
High Street, Lerwick, 72
Highland Light Infantry, 56, 59, 60
Hill 70 (place), 17, 67
Hill, John, 15
Hillside, Bressay, 54
Hillwell, Dunrossness, 56
Holland, 49
Hospital, 17, 22, 24-26, 30, 35, 36, 40,
    48, 53, 56, 62-65, 68, 76
Hoswick, Sandwick, 58
Huddleston, Sir Hubert Jervoise, 37, 39
Hunter, John, 9

Indians, 84
Influenza, 32
Inkster, Jimmy, 28
Internment, 49
Invergordon, 75
Ireland, Bigton, 72
Irvine, George, 55, 56
Irvine, Henry, 56
Isle of Man, 45
Isles of Thule (poem), 29

J.F., 49
Jamieson, Andrew, 50
Jamieson, Coventry, 50
Jamieson, James, 74-86
Jamieson, James Scott, 50
Jamieson, Peter, 74-86
Jamieson, Robert, 74-86
Jamieson, Robert W., 17
Jebel Marra, 38
Jebel Midob, 36
Jellicoe, Admiral, 54
Jellicoe, Lady Gwendoline, 54
Jericho, 70
Johnsen, Captain, 51
Johnson, Bobbie, 75
Johnson, James, 21
Johnson, Magnie, 75
Johnston, George, 73
Johnstone, James, 20
Jordan Valley, 70
Juba, 38, 40
Jutland, Battle of, 54

Kabga, 40
Kamloops, 24
Keila, 38
Kent, H.M.S., 46, 47
Kenya, 62
Khartoum, 35-37, 43
Khor Gabra, 39
Khors, 38, 39
King Harald Street, Lerwick, 32
Kordofan, 36, 37
Kulkul, 38

La Cateau, Battle of, 9

Lamont, Revd D., 67

Lanao, s.s., 51

Law, Bonar, 28

Law Lane, Lerwick, 45

Laxfirth, Tingwall, 18

Leask, Freddie, 78

Leask, Lawrence, 16

Leask, Mrs, 16

Lerwick, 9, 11-13, 15, 17, 19, 20, 22, 26, 28, 29, 32, 46, 50- 52, 56, 59, 62, 68-70, 72, 74,

Leslie, Margaret, 18

Letters, mail, parcels, and post office, 11, 14, 15, 18, 26, 30, 32, 33, 37, 38, 40, 41, 47, 49, 50, 53, 54, 58, 60, 64, 71, 75-77, 79, 82-84

Lifeboats, 50, 51, 53

Little Willie (shell), 13

Liverpool, 26, 30

Lofoten, s.s., 52

London, 79

Longhill, 50

Loos, Battle of, 15-17, 67

Lothian and Berwickshire Yeomanry, 67

Louveral Wood, 71

Louvre Disc (signalling), 74, 76

Lusitania, 12

Lyddite, 63

MacBean, D., 70

MacDonald, Mary Ann, 32

MacKay, Elizabeth, 18

MacKay, Trooper, 69

Machine guns, 10, 40, 14, 20, 23, 46, 58, 60, 69, 70

Mafurtac, 67

Mail (see Letters etc.)

Mainland, Henry, 51

Malaria, 35

Malta, 50

Manila, 51

Manson, James, 17

Maxims (see machine guns)

Measles, 64

Medical Hall, Lerwick, 20

Mediterranean, 35, 56

Mill Road Infirmary, 26

Mines, 16, 19-21, 52, 56, 58,

Minnewerfer (mortar), 20

Monroe, Sir Hector, 76

Morton, David (poet), 26, 29

Motherwell, 17

Nahud, 35, 40

Neuve Chapelle, 62, 63

Neven-Spence, Sir Basil , 34-43

Newlands, Jock, 75, 76

Nicolson, Artie, 75, 76

Nigg, 75

No Man's Land, 22, 25

North Shields, 53

North Wales, s.s., 47

Northern Patrol, 40

Nottingham, 14

Nursing, 61-65

Old Bill & Co., 77

Ollaberry, 24, 29

Ord Pinders Circus, 74

Orkney, 50

Palestine, 58, 70

Parcels (see Letters, etc.)

Paris, 30

Pears, Rear-Admiral Sir Edmund Radcliffe, 76

Penny, A., 69

Penzance, 47

Peterson, Jack, 26, 27, 30

Peterson, James, 19

Peterson, James snr., 19

Peterson, John (see Peterson, Jack)

Peterson, Lieut. D., 68, 69

Petrie, James Andrew, 67

Petrie, Laurence, 66, 67

Petrie, P.T., 67

Philippines, 51

Pilot Lane, Lerwick, 69

Pneumonia, 52, 64, 68

Porteous, William Thomas, 29

Portsmouth, 46

Portugal, 51

Post office (see Letters, etc.)

Postcard (see Mail etc.)

Pottinger, Tommy, 84

Prisoners, 12, 16, 22, 37, 39, 47, 48

Private Pat (See Peterson, Jack)

Punjab, 41

Ratter, J.D., 77

Rifle, 10, 11, 13, 17, 20, 23, 26, 31, 40, 58, 59, 63, 64, 69

Robertson, A., 45

Robertson, Magnus, 30

Rouen, 30

Royal Army Medical Corps (R.A.M.C.), 35, 75

Royal Flying Corps, 37

Royal Garrison Artillery, 32

Royal Naval Reserve, 44, 45, 49, 68

Royal Red Cross Medal, 62

Royal Scots, 9, 15, 58

Rücker, Claus, 50

Ruhleben Hospital, 48

Salt Lake Plain, 67

Salvation Army, 80

Sandbags, 13

Sandwick, 26

Sausage (mortar), 20

Scott, Captain John, 50, 70

Scott, James Moffat, 50

Scott, McGowan, 50

Scott, Thomas Moffat, 66, 70

Scottish Churches Hut, 80, 81

Scottish Fusiliers, 16

Scottish Horse, 67

Scottish Rifles, 11, 75

Seaforth Highlanders, 14, 22, 26, 75, 80-85

Senussi, 40

Shavau, 38

Sherwood Foresters, 13

Shrapnel, 24, 25, 30, 47, 60, 63, 69

Sinclair, Jamie, 28

Slater, William, 48

Smallpox, 37, 39

Smith, Capt. Malcolm, 58

Smith, Sir Malcolm , 58

Snipers, 17, 20, 24, 25, 69

Somme, 20, 21, 28

Spence, Andrew, 71

Spence, William T., 66, 71

St. Magnus Street, Lerwick, 74

St. Rognvald, s.s., 50, 70

Start Point, 52

Stout family, 22, 51

Stout, James, 22

Stretchers etc., 19, 21, 22, 24, 62, 63

Stronsay, 50

Submarines, 47, 50-53

Sudan, 34-43

Sumit, 38, 40

Sunken Road, 23

Sutherland, Archibald, 58

Sutherland, Donald, 26

Sutherland, Margaret, 58

Suvla Bay, 47

Talberts, Major F., 70

Tamad el Kedada, 39

Telegram/Telegraph, 68, 75, 79

Telephones, 15, 16, 75, 79

Thomas, Edward (poet), 29

Thomas, William Beach, 30

Tobacco (see cigarettes etc.)

Torpedoes, 45, 47, 51-53

Trenches, 10-11, 13-24, 29, 57-60, 64, 67-69, 82

Tresta, Aithsting, 73

Trindade, Battle of, 45

Tromp, s.s., 51, 52

Trondra, 48

U.S.A. (and entry in war), 51, 75, 78, 84

U-34, 50

U-39, 53

UB-38, 52

U-Boat (see submarines)

Uhlans, 18

Ulsta, Yell, 45

Unst, 67

Valencia, 52

Vancouver, 18, 24

Vandeleur, Major T.B., 37, 40

Vimy Ridge, 18, 24, 25

W. Coupland and Co., 52

Wad el Sheikh, 39

Wadbister, 10

Ward, William, 24

White, Tommy, 81

Whizz Bang (shell), 15, 22, 23

Williamson, Andrew, 72

Williamson, Barbara Ann, 74-86

Williamson, Robert, 66, 72

Withall, Martha, 62

Woodbines (see cigarettes etc.)

Woolwich, 22

Wounds, 9, 13, 14, 17-19, 21-26, 28,
   30, 37, 39, 40, 46, 50, 54, 56, 59,
   62-65, 69, 70, 72, 74

Y.M.C.A., 77, 80-82
Yeats, W.B., 30

Yei, 35
Yell, 45, 71
Yeomanry, 58, 67
Ypres, 10, 47

Zeebrugge, 45